WITHDRAWN
FROM
COLLECTION

FORDHAM
UNIVERSITY
LIBRARIES

D1522506

Australian Realism
The Systematic Philosophy of John Anderson

This book outlines the realist and pluralist philosophy of John Anderson, Australia's most original thinker, whose articles and teaching at Sydney University have deeply influenced Australian intellectual life. Several main themes run through his work, but Anderson never gave an overall account of his views. This is remedied here: in exhibiting the range of Anderson's thought, from logic, epistemology and theory of mind, to language and social theory, Baker's work sketches realism as a systematic philosophical position, and shows something of the history of ideas in Australia.

This book will be of particular interest to historians of modern philosophy, and those studying realism.

This world, which is the same for all, no one of gods or men has made; but it was ever, is now, and ever shall be an ever-living Fire, with measures kindling, and measures going out.

If you do not expect the unexpected, you will not find it; for it is hard to be sought out and difficult.   *Heraclitus*

Australian Realism
The Systematic Philosophy of John Anderson

A. J. BAKER

With an introduction by
ANTHONY QUINTON

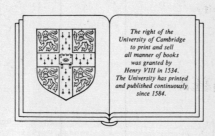

The right of the
University of Cambridge
to print and sell
all manner of books
was granted by
Henry VIII in 1534.
The University has printed
and published continuously
since 1584.

CAMBRIDGE UNIVERSITY PRESS

Cambridge
London   New York   New Rochelle
Melbourne   Sydney

Published by the Press Syndicate of the University of Cambridge
The Pitt Building, Trumpington Street, Cambridge CB2 1RP
32 East 57th Street, New York, NY 10022, USA
10 Stamford Road, Oakleigh, Melbourne 3166, Australia

© Cambridge University Press 1986

First published 1986

Printed in Great Britain by
Redwood Burn Limited, Trowbridge, Wiltshire

British Library cataloguing in publication data
Baker, A. J.
Australian realism: the systematic philosophy
of John Anderson.
1. Anderson, John, *1893–1962*
I. Title
199.94   B5704.A/

Library of Congress cataloguing in publication data
Baker, A. J.
Australian realism.
1. Anderson, John, 1893–   – Contributions in
realism.   2. Realism – History – 20th century.
I. Title.
B5704.A634B34   1986   199'.94   85–22383

ISBN 0 521 32051 8

Fordham University
LIBRARY
AT
LINCOLN CENTER
New York, N. Y.

B
5704
A6 B35
1986

Cop . 2

RB

Contents

Introduction

Australian philosophy has benefited enormously from the fact that it was dominated by John Anderson for the greater part of his active career and it is entirely just that the only one of the twelve chapters of S. A. Grave's *History of Australian Philosophy* that is devoted to a single philosopher is devoted to him. According to Grave, Australia's first philosopher was installed in 1850, but the interval between that date and 1927, when Anderson arrived from Scotland, is passed over in a couple of chapters. It is really due to Anderson that there is enough in Australian philosophy to write about at book length. The impulse of his powerful mind and resolute personality has been effectively kept up by his many distinguished pupils, notably J. A. Passmore and J. L. Mackie, and by their pupils in turn. It really is the same impulse, too, even if the philosophers who can be seen as following him by no means take over his doctrines wholesale. What they have more conspicuously got from him is an Andersonian spirit which combines business-like force and economy in tackling problems with ambitious boldness in taking on large topics and in seeing them as hanging together as parts of a single intellectual enterprise. Anderson's prose is a fit vehicle for thought of his sinewy, enterprising kind and it is something his followers have admirably kept up.

A convenient way of bringing out Anderson's large place in, and service to, Australian philosophy is to compare Australian philosophy with the philosophy of more populous and equally prosperous Canada. There have been some worthy Canadian philosophers – John Watson, expositor of Kant, and G. S. Brett, historian of psychology, for example – but none in Anderson's time who came anywhere near him in originality and importance. Nor, since his time, has there been any distinctively national excellence in Canadian philosophy. (The Canadian mind, it should be added, has plenty of extraphilosophical achievements to its credit: for instance, the economic history of H. A. Innis and the criticism of Northrop Frye.)

Anderson's belief in the systematic nature of philosophy or, more broadly, of the general interconnectedness of all branches of intellectual activity was a service to Australia as a whole and not just to Australian philosophy. His influence as a teacher, as an example of how the life of the mind should be carried on, has been felt and acknowledged by many Australians working outside the domain of philosophy proper: historians, psychologists, social theorists, literary critics. In the depressed and fairly repressive 1930s he was a valuable public nuisance of the Socratic variety, keeping independence of thought alive at a time when there was much to frighten people out of it.

On the other hand, Anderson owed a lot to Australia and, in a way, to Australian philosophy, or, at any rate, to a philosopher of Australian birth. A powerful influence was exerted on him by the Gifford lectures delivered in Glasgow towards the end of the first world war by Samuel Alexander, later published as *Space, Time and Deity*. Alexander, born in Sydney, had graduated in Melbourne and gone to England to become the first Jewish tutor in an Oxford college and, later on, professor of philosophy at Manchester. Anderson was strongly attracted by Alexander's conception of philosophy as descriptive or factual, as a kind of general science, and by his realism, by his unwillingness to countenance any sort of existence but natural existence in space and time. On a more pedestrian level, it seems that Alexander played some part in getting Anderson his first job at Sydney.

What Anderson got from Australia in general was opportunity. It was philosophically more or less virgin soil, highly inviting to someone who lived up to his own high valuation of creative adventurousness. His particular force of intellect and will meant that for a long time he had no serious competition to face. He was able to dominate the abler young philosophers and could cope easily with the local criticism excited by his innovations and impieties, which provided him with just the right

amount of roughage to keep his critical digestion in good working order.

It is an advantage for an original thinker to get on with working his ideas out in an uncluttered environment, with some
praise and interest to keep his enthusiasm alive, some manage-
able criticism to keep him on his toes, but with not too many
clever people breathing discouragingly down his neck. A well
formed and thickly populated intellectual scene can have a dis-
abling effect on a philosopher taking his first steps. Indeed once
Anderson himself was established as unquestionable philosophical leader, his own pupils were deterred from all but more or less
parenthetical or marginal publication, either footnoting his doctrines or moving off into regions like the scholarly history of philosophy to which he laid no imperial claim.

Anderson's rapid ascent to being king of the hitherto modest
castle of Australian philosophy certainly encouraged him to
work out his new and powerful ideas in a wide-ranging and
enterprising fashion. But the measure of isolation from the
English-speaking philosophical community at large that enabled
him to make such an impressive start set up a habit of intellectual self-sufficiency that was bad for him, since it exempted his
ideas from the serious criticism which, once safely brought to
maturity, they could have profited from. It was also a misfortune
for English-speaking philosophy generally that his ideas, which
were never published in book form until 1962, the year of his
death, were almost wholly confined in print to Australian
periodicals, above all to the *Australasian Journal of Psychology
and Philosophy*, which soon became almost the house organ of
the Andersonian school. The only exceptions are a couple of discussion notes in *Mind* in 1926, in which he criticises F. C. S.
Schiller's rejection of F. H. Bradley's theory of truth on the
ground that both of them fail to acknowledge the objective truth
of ordinary propositions, and an important paper, in the *Proceedings of the Aristotelian Society* for 1926/7, 'The Knower and
the Known', setting out his refutation of the Cartesian conceptions, deeply rooted in nearly all subsequent western philosophy, of the mind as simply a consciousness and of its objects as

no more than its own sense-impressions. Unsupported by other available writings these first utterances failed to secure any attention in the place of their first publication. The first serious notice I know of that his thoughts received by a philosopher outside Australia was the characteristically breezy compound of endorsement and correction contained in Gilbert Ryle's 'Logic and Professor Anderson' in the *Australasian Journal* for 1950.

Since 1962 general awareness of Anderson's thought has greatly increased. Passmore and Mackie, his most able and productive pupils, have written authoritatively about him at article length and have spread the word further by more or less definite references to their indebtedness to him. D. Z. Phillips, in *Education and Inquiry*, has edited a selection of Anderson's educational writings. A. J. Baker, in *Anderson's Social Philosophy*, has surveyed Anderson's social and political thought and practice. In the present book he has gone on to give a rounded and comprehensive account of the whole range of Anderson's philosophy. It has the special authority that comes from its being the work of a pupil and close associate. The task of an introduction in these circumstances is to look at the connection of Anderson's somewhat enclosed and self-sufficient body of ideas with the general movement of philosophy in his epoch outside the area where for long it lay largely concealed from general view.

The central elements of Anderson's philosophy are his more or less cosmological doctrine of empirical realism, his more or less logical doctrine, which might be called factualism, (qualified as more or less cosmological and logical respectively because Anderson would have admitted no such contrast, for him logic, or its basic part, *is* cosmology) and his doctrine, argumentatively crucial, that relations presuppose qualities, that nothing can be related to anything else unless both have in addition non-relational qualities.

Anderson's empirical realism is ordinarily expressed in the formula that there is only one way of being, the way in question being spatio-temporal. Everything that there is exists in space and time; there are no abstract or eternal objects; minds are part of nature and in space; values are natural qualities of human activities, or of the social movements in which human activities are carried on. A host of arguments is invoked to support this position, most notably the impossibility of putting together the realms of being that misguided philosophers have been led to put asunder – Passmore calls it the two-worlds argument in the chapter of his *Philosophical Reasoning* devoted to it. Symptomatic of this impossibility are the irreducible problems of explaining how particulars can conceivably participate in universals and of how mind and body, Cartesianly dualised, can interact as they evidently do in perception and in acts of will.

In this work of ontological deflation, to borrow Ryle's term, Anderson is at one with a number of twentieth century philosophers. One of them, indeed, is Ryle himself, whose writings on philosophical logic and the philosophy of mind have been single-mindedly devoted to the elimination, respectively, of reified abstractions and of private inner states, of logical and mental entities with a 'special status' outside the observable natural world in space and time. Anderson's position has much in common, too, with the reism of Kotarbinski which affirms that only objects, conceived in a straightforward, observable, spatio-temporal way, exist and that properties and the like, on the one hand, and experiences and the like, on the other, are not objects. D. C. Williams, in the essays that make up his *Principles of Empirical Realism*, argues for a similar view, even if, in the end, he interprets concrete objects as complexes of 'tropes' or abstract particulars.

Anderson associates his reistic principle that there is only one way of being, that of common objects in space and time, with the principle that there is only one way of knowing or, one might also say, only one way of speaking (if, at any rate, one is actually going to say anything). To know anything is to know some matter of actual fact and to say anything is to describe, or misdescribe, such a matter of fact. This second, epistemic or logical, principle does not obviously follow from the first, cosmological principle. That all factual knowledge is of natural facts and that all descriptive discourse is about observable things in space and time does not obviously imply that all knowledge is factual or that all adequate discourse is descriptive.

Two obtrusively apparent counter-examples are *a priori* knowledge (in logic, mathematics and perhaps philosophy itself) and judgements of value. Platonism takes *a priori* knowledge as having universals for its objects and their eternal relationships as its content, matters, that is to say, of abstract, non-natural fact. Ethical intuitionism takes an analogous line about values. But the existence of *a priori* knowledge and of significant value-judgements can be admitted by those who believe in Anderson's single way of being if they understand the former as conceptual and the latter either as describing complex, but still natural characteristics of mental life, or as not descriptive at all but as appropriated to another significant employment such as commanding or commending.

Anderson's claim that the truths of logic and mathematics describe matters of natural fact starts from the relatively plausible, and frequently seductive, idea that geometry is the science of space. His claim becomes less plausible when he goes on to say that the logical relation of implication is a 'sensible relation'. Generally sensible relations have objects as their terms. Implication, however, relates propositions (or, Anderson might prefer to say, facts). In claiming that the truths of logic are simply very general pieces of natural description he fastens on their role as propositions at the expense of what many would see as their more fundamental role as rules of inference (or, more precisely, as the propositional correlates of such rules). There is little temptation to construe what are primarily rules as descriptions. He would reject the view that they are analytic on the ground that propositions true by definition are not really propositions at all, but rather degenerate, proposition-like forms of words. But proof in logic and mathematics is either by inference from premises which it is evidently contradictory to deny or is accomplished by *reductio ad absurdum*, by inferring a contradiction from the denial of the proposition to be proved. In either case the inferences which compose the argument correspond to logical truths it would be evidently contradictory to deny. Why should what is got from sub-propositions by sub-propositional means be supposed to be substantially, descriptively prop-

ositional? There is, no doubt, an affinity between Anderson's
rejection of the *a priori* and Quine's of the analytic. But it is a
remote one. For Quine the truths of logic and mathematics are
at the outer, minimally factual end of a continuum; for Anderson every proposition is as straightforwardly, literally and
uncompromisingly factual as every other.

Anderson's unconcern with inference comes out again in what
he has to say about science, which is something he tends to
regard from the corner of his eye, since he has no explicit philosophy of science. He denies that scientific hypotheses are
inferred inductively from singular reports of observation on the
traditionally logical ground that singular propositions are a
species of universal propositions: 'Socrates is mortal' being as
much a universal affirmative as 'all men are mortal'. He holds
that causal generalities are simple descriptions of what we
observe, as much as reports of the shape or colour of things,
even if more risky. There are, as he sees it, no essentially
inferred propositions and also, it would seem, no essentially
inferred objects. He does not appear to acknowledge any problem about theoretical entities. This is an aspect of his general
repudiation of ultimates. Axiomatic first principles and basic
empirical propositions are rejected along with absolute simples
and totalities. Just as everything is complex and has parts, on the
one hand, and is a part of something more complex than itself,
on the other, so every proposition may be inferred from others
or be the basis of an inference to others.

Anderson's account of judgements of value or, as he might
prefer to put it, of value facts and the knowledge we have of
them, is not entirely idiosyncratic. He takes the goodness of the
things that are good, namely certain human activities, to be a
straightforwardly describable property of those things. So far he
is at one with G. E. Moore. But he disagrees with Moore in
taking the property of goodness to be a natural one. Like Moore
he goes on to reveal what it is that he finds as a matter of fact to
be good. His catalogue turns out to have a more vigorous flavour
than Moore's: activities are good to the extent that they are free,
creative, productive, enterprising, risky.

Another difference from Moore embodies Anderson's most profound ethical idiosyncrasy: his complete detachment of the good from the right. Moore had linked them by definition: the right act was the one that had better results than any available alternative. For Anderson, while the good is a matter of discoverable natural fact, talk of what is right is a misleading way of talking about what is required or commanded, which misleads by failing to mention the requirer or commander. It is interesting to see how Anderson just manages, in his hostility to what he calls moralism, to avoid saying that his readers *ought* to do or think anything, while leaving it perfectly clear that he has firm designs on their conduct and beliefs.

There are anticipatory glimpses in what Anderson has to say about mind, of what has come to be called Australian materialism. But he did not feel impelled to explain just how mind is located in space, as it has to be on his view of it. He was more concerned to argue that there has to be more to mind than the merely relational characteristic of consciousness. The indispensable qualitative element of mind he saw as feeling or emotion, an idea for which he claimed Freudian support, as he did also for his bold denial of the indurated prejudice that the mind or self is a unity, even a 'simple substance'. To him the mind or self is a society of interacting, and indeed conflicting, emotions. Society proper, as a collection of interacting selves, is a complex of very much the same sort, even if writ a good deal larger, in firm opposition to the reductive pieties of liberal individualism, for which the individual is real or substantial, society an abstraction or construction.

In his social theory his factualism combines with his account of the self and his rejection of moralism to provide something new and unusual, even if he admitted a debt to Sorel. Society is a scene of conflict, not so much between individual human beings as between the social movements and institutions on which human beings depend for the humanly distinctive characteristics they have. There is no such thing as the common good and no necessity about progress, indeed there is perhaps no possibility of it, if it is taken to be the continuous enhancement of the common good. Anderson applies these ideas to education and fiercely opposes education for citizenship or social adjustment in the interests of what he sees as true education, the acquisition of habits of critical inquiry and of independence of mind. If it is none too clear how his committed endorsement of non-utilitarian education is able, on his principles, to pass as a strictly theoretical description of social fact, it is abundantly clear what he himself favours.

Anderson's views about most of the central topics of philosophy and many major topics in the surrounding intellectual country form a system, held together by a definite style of thought. System, for Anderson, is the prime virtue of Hegel, whom he takes to be its greatest exponent, for all his faults in other respects. Anderson's ideas are refreshingly bold and original and are sustained by fertile and tenacious argumentation. For all his emphasis on description his philosophical practice is indefatigably inferential. His doctrines and the reasoning that supports them challenge the reader who comes on them for the first time. They do not invite, and are unlikely to get, unquestioning acceptance. But at the very least it is invigorating to wrestle with them. Their constitutional force is such that they cannot be quietly contemplated from a distance. Whether one accepts his views or rejects them, the business of coming to terms with them is one which makes one's thoughts markedly different afterwards from what they were when one first embarked on it.

ANTHONY QUINTON
Trinity College, Oxford

Preface

John Anderson, 1893–1962, studied philosophy in Glasgow University under members of a flourishing idealist school that had been established by Edward Caird in the latter part of the nineteenth century. It was one of Caird's Glasgow students and another idealist, Francis Anderson, who became Sydney University's first Professor of Philosophy in 1890. However, John Anderson received a powerful stimulus towards realism when he heard Samuel Alexander give his Gifford Lectures in Glasgow in 1916–17, and he began to work out his own realism while lecturing in the 1920s in Edinburgh University. But it was in Sydney University, where he was Challis Professor of Philosophy from 1927 to 1958, that he developed, and wrote in detail on, his own far-reaching realist position.

Alexander was born in Sydney (he left Australia in his late teens) and Professor Passmore has speculated (in *A Hundred Years of Philosophy*) that Alexander's opposition to idealist Absolutism had a connection with the 'democratic' spirit of his Australian origins. That is a feasible view, though Anderson once speculated in a different way when he suggested that, while the Australian is commonly regarded as having a stoical or philosophical temperament, this is really 'an attitude of mere apathy and indifference, of acquiescence in the vagaries of an environment which one cannot master', as distinct from 'the strictly philosophical recognition of the fact that things have their own ways of working'. However, even on that view one can argue for a connection with the realist movement which developed around Anderson in that the force of that movement and its tough-minded approach obviously flowed in part from the need to surmount the harsh environment and prevailing intellectual apathy. Perhaps, too, I can suggest (as will please partisans of the theory that the spiritual climate of Sydney differs sharply from that of places like Melbourne) that the abrasive life and outlook of Sydney was conducive to the abrasive, uncompromising approach of Anderson and his followers.

Apart from Alexander, Anderson was not quite the first Sydney realist as his predecessor in the Sydney Chair, Bernard Muscio (who died at the early age of thirty-nine), while he had studied under Francis Anderson in Sydney, went on at Cambridge to become a supporter of the New Realism that was then developing. However, this was revealed in some good articles Muscio wrote in the period around 1914, rather than in his teaching at Sydney University in the 1920s, and it was left to John Anderson to sponsor realism as a serious philosophical force in Australia.

At any rate, Anderson went on to become the most original, all-round philosopher Australia has had, and to have a striking influence through his teaching, his many articles in local journals, the enthusiasm of his followers, and his contributions at Australian philosophy conferences. With regard to those conferences, from 1939 on, when G. A. Paul and later D. A. T. Gasking and A. C. Jackson – all former students of Wittgenstein at Cambridge – came to teach philosophy in Melbourne University, the conferences became particularly alive and provided impressive contrasts in style and doctrine between Sydney 'Andersonians' and Melbourne 'Wittgensteinians'.

Anderson influenced many students who went on to become philosophers or to specialise in various other disciplines or professions. But despite his influence his philosophical views have never been made widely known, even in Australia, nor have they ever been discussed as fairly and fully as they deserved. Of the several reasons for this, one is that he never worked out his position thoroughly, in part because he was an active educator and controversialist, but also because he was not very responsive to the need for detailed elaboration. Despite his belief in the value of *movements* and his sometimes saying that members of them, including members of 'movements one could name', would be wise to be prepared to extend and criticise their founder's views, the fact is that he was quite possessive about his philosophy and discouraged or inhibited members of his school from themselves working and writing on core parts of his position. So the able people who were close in spirit to his thought either wrote little, or, in their writing, avoided tackling central issues. In some ways Anderson was quite opposed to publicising his philosophy – except by the medium of lecturing to his students and writing articles mainly directed at members of his school; although a part defence of this is found in his belief that a philosophical position can only be grasped by concentrated study of it, and in his lack of interest in the embourgeoisement of his views or their becoming fashionable for the wrong reasons. It is noteworthy that when Gilbert Ryle wrote to Anderson to ask if he would care to write for *Mind* he was uninterested, and when Ryle wrote a provocative article in *The Australasian Journal of Philosophy* criticising his views, Anderson did not deign to reply (except in part of a posthumously published essay), although the occasion was a good one for clarifying and publicising his views to what would have been a large and interested set of readers.

The 1962 collection of Anderson's articles is now long out of print, and in any case many of his articles are somewhat opaque to readers outside his school. Apart from Ryle, who clearly made some mistakes in his account of Anderson's position, I recall for example George Paul (who was one of my post-Sydney teachers at Oxford) pointing out to me that he found it hard to understand some of Anderson's writings, such as on causality. Consequently, this book is intended to fill the need for a clear, detailed statement of Anderson's overall position and of how he argues for it. That is why, while I do raise difficulties and develop criticisms here and there, I have concentrated on trying to communicate, in an organised way, the nature of his various views. That is why too, because of the greater difficulty of understanding that may arise for the reader in the case of logic, I have left Anderson's formal logic until a later chapter – instead of, as would be the most systematic approach, beginning with it. In my presentation I have, of course, given priority to what Anderson himself wrote or said, but I have also drawn on the general teaching of his school, and where necessary I have reconstructed missing views or arguments in a way that I believe is consonant with his position.

I should like to thank Dr Paul Foulkes, who also studied under John Anderson, for his help and advice.

Recurrent abbreviations used are as follows.

Studies	John Anderson, *Studies in Empirical Philosophy*, Angus and Robertson Ltd, Sydney, 1962.
A.J.P.P.	*The Australasian Journal of Psychology and Philosophy*
A.J.P.	*The Australasian Journal of Philosophy* (which became the name of the *A.J.P.P.* in 1947)

The '*Anderson Archive*' refers to the collection of Anderson's lecture notes and other material that is located in the Archivist's section of Fisher Library, University of Sydney.

The quotations from Heraclitus on the title page are taken from John Burnet's *Early Greek Philosophy*. The quotations at the beginning of each chapter are taken from Anderson's writings.

A. J. BAKER

I
Realism

Realism is a pluralistic doctrine or theory of independence.

The fact that discussion is advanced by consideration only of *the issue itself*, and not of the persons who hold views about it, is evidence of the truth of the realistic position.

ANDERSON'S REALISM

Realism is a description that applies to Anderson's general or overall position,[1] including what we can call his 'ontological egalitarianism'. According to this, *whatever exists* – combustion machines, polar ice-caps, wattle leaves, human enterprise; the mental and the non-mental; the 'important' and the 'trivial'; the permanent and the ephemeral – is real, that is to say it is a spatial and temporal situation or occurrence that is on *the same level of reality* as anything else that exists.

In addition to that, realism embraces more particular aspects of his philosophy, including his realistic view of logic, of universality, and of *knowledge*.

This last view – which is commonly equated with 'realism' in a narrow sense – is a theory of 'naive' or 'common sense' or 'direct' realism according to which, despite the occurrence of errors and illusions (a fact exploited and exaggerated by Descartes and his anti-realist successors), we can and very often do know or observe real trees, tables, or what some philosophers call 'material' things or objects. This plain man's view of

[1] Anderson oscillated between *realism* and *empiricism* (he regarded them as virtually the same position) as the best description of his general position. Thus, he sharply contrasts empiricism with rationalism but also maintains that 'The real object of realist attack is rationalism' ('Realism', *The Australian Highway*, 1958, p. 54). I have opted for realism as the best description, because of its association with objectivism, another key part of his philosophy, and because the term 'empiricism' has the disadvantage that it is frequently used to convey views that are at variance with Anderson's empiricism.

knowledge was philosophically revived and defended by the movement known as *modern realism* which flourished in Britain, and to a lesser extent in America, in the first part of this century in reaction to the then dominant doctrines of philosophical idealism. G. E. Moore and Bertrand Russell were important early members of this movement, though they later developed other views, as were the American *New Realists*, especially W. T. Marvin and R. B. Perry, and Samuel Alexander. The movement profited too from the work of John Burnet on Greek philosophy and of Sigmund Freud on psychoanalysis. Anderson himself was influenced by all of these writers, especially by Alexander, and also by some of the work of the American William James. Anderson was, however, critical of various unrealistic elements in the thinking of the modern realists, including Alexander, and went on himself to put forward, in his teaching and writing in Australia, the most systematic and thoroughgoing realist position that has ever been developed.

But to start with the initial modern realist position, this involved to some extent, as is true of any abiding philosophical controversy, dogmatic counter assertion by the realists against the assertions then dominant – though, as Anderson said, they were certainly not *more dogmatic* than their opponents. However, the realists also backed up their claims by *argument*, including powerful criticisms of competing views of knowledge: representative perception, idealism and sense-data views.

The theory of representative perception (which I will merely sketch and then outline the realists' criticism) is associated in the history of philosophy with a main strand in the philosophy of John Locke. According to it, the mind directly contemplates mental occurrences or 'ideas' that represent or correspond to material objects (or fail to correspond to them in the case of error), but these material objects cannot be directly contemplated. I have direct knowledge of an idea of a tree or a table but only indirect knowledge of the tree or table itself. But this theory, while it has been popular amongst scientists, is regarded by most philosophers as subject to insuperable difficulties. Thus, for example, if we have no direct knowledge of material objects how can we refer to them as resembling or giving rise to ideas, and why should we even suppose that there are material things at all? As Anderson puts it, against a 'picture-copy' variant of the theory (put forward by Lenin), 'in order to show that "an idea" is a good or bad copy of "an external thing", we should have to know them both and compare them – but, of course if we can know external things directly, then the whole picture-theory collapses.'[2] As this criticism illustrates, the realist technique of argument against the representationist is to show that he is involved in an unavoidable inconsistency, resolution of which entails accepting realism. Take again his claim that we cannot know a tree directly but only an idea of it; if that is so a consistent campaign against direct knowledge would lead him to say that we cannot know the idea directly either, but only an idea of an idea, and so on for ever – which reveals that the representationist does accept direct knowledge when it suits him; and that, of course, is what he also does when he blithely assumes that the trees to which our ideas are judged to correspond are there, available for comparison with ideas.

Rejection of this theory sets the background to the idealist – realist controversy. Idealists from Berkeley onwards all dismissed representative perception as a viable view and sought to repair its deficiencies by eliminating material things altogether and maintaining that whatever exists is mental.

ABSOLUTE IDEALISM

The most powerful form of idealism is 'absolute' or 'Hegelian' or 'objective' idealism which was the dominant western philosophy for most of the nineteenth century and well into the twentieth century, and indeed was probably the most influential philosophy that has ever been in vogue in its own time. It was effectively presented in Britain by a variety of writers, T. H. Green, E. Caird, B. Bosanquet and especially F. H. Bradley, and it was against this philosophy that the realists reacted.

Idealism's most famous claim is that ordinary things or 'out-

[2] *Studies*, pp. 299–300.

side objects' (apart from other minds) depend for their existence on being known – their *esse* is *percipi*, or in Bradley's words 'Reality is experience'. That is to say, tables, buildings, mountains and so on would not exist if there were no minds (including Absolute Mind) to be conscious of or experience them.

It was this claim, and the counter realist claim that what is known is not constituted by or dependent for its existence on being known, that generated most attention in the idealist–realist controversy, but as many idealists – and Anderson notably amongst realists – saw, this is only *one* of the issues in the controversy and is not the philosophically most important one. Thus, the view that 'Reality is experience' is very closely connected in idealist thought with claims about the nature and grading of reality and about the nature of relations (and not merely the relation of knowing or experiencing), as follows.

1 There is a fundamental contrast (a *metaphysical* or *ontological* contrast) between on the one hand 'ultimate reality', what really is and gives philosophical and moral significance to existence, and on the other hand 'appearances' or 'brute facts' which make up the 'world' as it ordinarily appears, the realm of common sense and (though science is an improvement on common sense) the realm of science. This is a wide claim which involves, as Anderson says, the idealist version of *rationalism*.

2 Ultimate reality is the 'One', 'Whole', 'Absolute' or 'Organic Unity'; it alone is really real, and any lesser existence – an aspect or part or moment of the One or Organic Whole – has a higher or lower *degree of reality* depending on the extent to which it embodies or approximates to the Absolute. Correspondingly, with regard to truth, a belief or judgement has a higher or lower *degree of truth* depending on how near it comes to (unattainable) absolute truth about the Absolute. It is the fusion of this conception of a single ultimate reality, that is, its *ontological monism*, with the knowledge thesis that 'Reality is experience', which gives power and complexity to this idealist system as compared, for example, with the more limited so-called 'subjective idealism' of Berkeley. It is because of this

fusion that Hegel and his followers speak so often and characteristically about Absolute Spirit, Reason or Consciousness.

3 There is the theory of constitutive or internal relations. According to this more obscure thesis, just as in the special case of knowledge the known thing is somehow constituted by being known or is really internal to the knower, so in the case of all other relations there are no merely 'external' or 'extrinsic' relations. Every relation involves the 'very nature of its terms', and when this is taken in conjunction with the doctrine of the One or Whole it follows that everything is inseparably connected with everything else, so that apparently separate relationships (Bradley cites for example the resemblance between two red-haired men and the spatial relation between a man and a billiard ball) are not separate at all – it is a form of 'vicious abstraction' so to regard them – and they can only be understood as manifestations of the underlying unity of the Absolute.

Now realist criticism, as advanced especially by Moore and Russell and later by Anderson, sets out to demolish each of these tenets of idealism. But having noticed the broad bases of idealism, its maintaining of 1, 2 and 3 in conjunction with the knowledge thesis, and the correspondingly broad nature of realist criticism, I will return now to that thesis and reserve until later chapters treatment of 1, 2 and 3.

IDEALISM ON KNOWLEDGE

In Anderson's view, as against the idealist theory of knowledge, the natural and common sense position to adopt and the one that all of us (including idealists) do in fact tacitly adopt is the realist position that minds and what they know are independently real things. So he asserts this as the true position and in support of it sets out to expose the philosophical errors that have misled idealists and induced them and their followers to find plausibility in their own claims to the contrary.

Anderson, in line with numerous other critics, notes that for the initial errors of idealism we have to go back to Descartes and his account of the *cogito* and of thought as an essence, and to the theory of ideas developed by his successors. That is, although idealists took their own position a long way beyond what Descartes and Berkeley for example maintained, nevertheless their position does assume certain basic contentions of Descartes and Berkeley; it was an unquestioning assumption of these contentions that gave Hegel and Bradley, for instance, the confidence to put forward their own more grandiose views.

Descartes advanced a well known ontological dualism of mind and matter according to which there are two utterly separate essential types of being, mental and material substance. But the dualism aside, the important legacy for modern idealism was, first, the view of mental substance as something whose essence consists in thinking (as is supposed to be established by the *cogito*) and the associated claim that all consciousness is self consciousness, and, second, the view, developed explicitly by Berkeley, that the objects of mind or consciousness, ideas or perceptions, are dependent existences whose being lies in being perceived.

Accordingly, in undermining the plausibility of the idealist case we can start by criticising these views of Descartes and Berkeley. Anderson does so in two ways. One, as will be made clearer later, consists in objecting to the very conception of consciousness as 'that whose nature it is to know' and of idea as 'that whose nature it is to be known'; each conception, he argues, involves *relativism* – which is his technical term for a confused amalgamation of a quality with a relation; consciousness is supposed to be the character of mind and at the same time the relation to that of which it is conscious; ideas are supposed to be essentially related to mind and at the same time to be the character or content of what is known.

In addition, he shows that Descartes's and Berkeley's basic 'demonstrations' in fact depend on making use of essences, identities and ambiguities. Thus, in the case of the *cogito*, Anderson's own neat contribution to the voluminous argumentation on the subject runs, in summary, as follows. Descartes's view is that *I think* is the one proposition that survives the doubting process because I cannot, without absurdity suppose that *I do not think*. This may be expressed, putting in brackets the proposition being tested, as: 'I think (that grass is green), but it is possible that grass is not green'; 'I think (that I think), but it is possible that I do not think', where the first is an acceptable formula but the latter is rejected as absurd, that is, it appears that it is necessary that I think. But, in fact, the absurdity attaching to the second formula depends, not on the bracketed *I think* but on the first *I think*, as is revealed by putting something else in brackets as in the formula, 'I think (that grass is green), but it is possible that I do not think', where the absurdity remains. Whereas if the first *I think* is replaced and we have, say, 'It is said (that I think), but it is possible that I do not think', there is no absurdity. In other words, Descartes has not tested *I think* at all but smuggled it in from the beginning.[3]

Likewise, Descartes's argument that all consciousness is self-consciousness, or that we always know ourselves as knowing, depends on a confusion which Anderson sums up as follows. 'The assumption is that we cannot suppose ourselves, in knowing, not to know, i.e., we cannot suppose that when we know, we do not know; but it is employed as if it meant that we cannot, in knowing, suppose ourselves not to know. Or, putting the argument positively, we must suppose ourselves, in knowing, to know; hence we must, in knowing, suppose ourselves to know (or, in thinking, think that we think).'[4] Similarly, in the case of Berkeley, he points out that his confidence in the obviousness of what he claims is in fact based on a confusion. 'Can there', he quotes Berkeley as asking, '*be* a nicer strain of abstraction than to distinguish the existence of sensible objects from their being perceived, so as to conceive them existing unperceived?' But Berkeley's argument amounts to passing from the bare identity 'What is perceived cannot be unperceived' to the conclusion that 'What is perceived cannot be perceived (or conceived or taken) to be perceived', that is, that 'What is perceived must be perceived to be perceived', which is an argument that depends on

---

[3] *Studies*, p. 103.   [4] *Studies*, p. 31.

the illicit substitution of 'perceived to be perceived' for 'perceived'.[5]

Arguments similar to those of Descartes and Berkeley
flourished in later idealist thought. So when realists sought to
advance their own views about knowledge – such as that 'things
known may continue to exist unaltered when they are not known
... or that the existence of a thing is not correlated with or dependent upon the fact that anybody experiences it, perceives it,
conceives it, or is in any way aware of it'[6] – they concentrated on
exposing the fallacious character of idealist arguments making
use of ambiguities in such terms as 'consciousness', 'subject',
'object' and 'content'. Thus Moore, in his seminal pioneer
article on 'The Refutation of Idealism',[7] raised the question of
what idealists meant when they talked about the 'content' of
consciousness or sensation (as when, for example, with reference to my seeing something blue, blue is said to be the content
of my sensation) and he went on to argue that their use of the
word 'content' enables them to confuse two quite separate
cases: (1) where, for example, blue is a content of my mind in
the way that blue is a content of a blue flower or a blue bead, and
(2) where blue is a 'content' in the sense of being an *object* of
which I am aware, that is, where I have quite different relation
to something blue, that of being aware *of* it. This confusion –
which is another instance of what Anderson calls *relativism*: in
(1) the 'content' is a quality and in (2) a non-predicative relation
– enables idealists to assume the mind-dependence of what is
known and at the same time to appear to account for the relation
the knower has to what he knows. But the two cases are quite
separate. What is asserted in (1) (that my consciousness *is* blue),
as Moore ironically notes, is unimportant and very likely false,
whereas (2), which is obviously true, presupposes that the blue
is 'an independent real thing', so that in being aware of it I am
already 'outside the circle of my own ideas and sensations'.[8]

[5] *Studies*, pp. 29–30.
[6] W. P. Montague, *The New Realism*, by E. B. Holt and five others, Macmillan,
New York, 1912, p. 474; quoted by Anderson, *Studies*, p. 27.
[7] In his *Philosophical Studies*, esp. pp. 21–30.
[8] Anderson criticised Moore for his own relativism in this article in using the

In an analogous way, Anderson criticises idealist claims about the interdependence of knower and known or, as they more often put it, of 'consciousness' and 'idea' or 'subject' and 'object'. Their argument characteristically proceeded by assuming that there was an 'opposition' or 'dualism' between subject and object which posed a problem about how they could be related. According to this, there is the difficulty that the object cannot be known if it *is* distinguished from the subject (for then it is not related to the subject) and it cannot be known if it is *not* distinguished from the subject (for then the two would be identical and there is still no relation). This opposition is then supposed to be overcome by means of the Hegelian principle of the 'identity of opposites' or 'unity in diversity': although subject and object are different this difference is overcome by their underlying identity or unity, and the agency by which this is done is the 'progressive realisation of self-consciousness'. A quotation from Edward Caird will illustrate.

The reason why the two terms, the self and the not-self, thus appear to be independent of each other, or to be brought together only as they externally act or react upon each other, lies in this, that the object is imperfectly known, and the subject is imperfectly self-conscious. This, however, does not make it less true that in self-consciousness is to be found the principle in reference to which the whole process may be explained . . . The dawn of consciousness, in which the external object first comes into existence for us, as opposed to self, is at the same time the beginning of the process by which its externality is negated or overcome.[9]

Anderson rejects idealist contentions of this kind by objecting to the supposed principle of identity involved and to its application to 'subjects' and 'objects'. Thus, as against the principle that apparent differences are really identities, he points out that

term 'awareness' to refer both to the relation of knowing and to what *has* the relation (*Studies*, p. 38n). He also deplored (Archive lecture notes on Moore) his later theory of 'sensibles' and his lack of a positive view of mind which, he argued, took Moore back, nearer and nearer to an an idealist position.

[9] *Essays on Literature and Philosophy*, James Maclehose and Sons, Glasgow, 1892, Vol. II, p. 470 and p. 472.

'If when we say that A is not B, we are somehow also saying that
A is B and B is A, discourse will be impossible.'[10] In other
words, differences are absolutely real as is presupposed by idealists themselves when they start to tell us about the differences
between subject and object that are to be 'overcome'. It is,
moreover, the use of words like 'subject' and 'object' that helps
idealists make it appear that there is an inseparable connection
between the mind and what it is aware of, for these words, of
course, are correlative ones. But, although whenever there is a
subject there must be a corresponding object and *vice versa*, it
by no means follows, if something A is a knowing subject related
to a known object B, that A and B are not independently real
things; as is plainly illustrated by a parallel case such as that of
marriage: although there is no husband without a wife and vice
versa, husband and wife are two different persons.

In this way, then, he argues that the realist will not be fazed by
arguments turning on ambiguities and obfuscations. There is a
whole set of words as well as 'subject' and 'object' – such as
'thought', 'consciousness', 'belief', 'knowledge', 'judgement',
'perception', 'sensation', 'experience' – unclear use of which has
lent plausibility to idealist and related positions. To illustrate by
reference to 'experience', when we speak of 'A's experience of
B' there are several things that may be meant: (1) the experien-
c*er* A, that is, what it is that is doing the experiencing, (2) the B
that is experienc*ed*, (3) the whole situation A's experiencing B,
and (4) the specific relation experienc*ing*. But to run these cases
together, Anderson is pointing out, is to be guilty of the error of
relativism; they can be clearly distinguished from one another;
and they provide no grounds at all for saying that A and B are
not two separate things.

SENSE-DATA VIEWS

By 1930 idealism was on the decline in Britain and America –
though it was still the philosophy taught by almost all Australian

[10] *Studies*, p. 42.

philosophers, which was partly why Anderson made such a powerful impact when he began to teach realism in Sydney and defend it at philosophy conferences. The idealist approach to knowledge was, however, continued in other ways, notably in the form of what is called *phenomenalism*, the adherents of which usually eschew sweeping idealist theses about the nature of reality, but do maintain that what we are immediately and basically aware of are *sense-data* (or sensa, sense-contents, sensibilia), for example, that when someone looks at a 'material object' such as a table he has sense-data of roundness, smoothness, brownness, and so on, but that while that is certainly the case it is a further question how, if at all, the material object can be analysed or accounted for in terms of sense-data.

Anderson rejected this position as making no advance at all on the arguments and assumptions of idealism, and he objected *in toto* to the view that there is a special kind of knowledge, *sensing*, and a special kind of object *sensa*. Thus, if *any* class of things consist of 'sensa' or 'sense-data' (Russell, for instance, at one time suggested that as well as the 'sensed' ones there were 'unsensed' sense-data) then, Anderson points out, 'to speak of knowing them as "sensing" is ... no more justifiable than to speak of knowing trees as "treeing"'.[11] Apart from that, in regard to the usual view that sense-data are private to, and known with certainty by, the persons who sense them, he points out that this view is open to criticisms similar to those that are applicable to idealism. Sense-data are more examples of 'dependent existences', entities 'whose nature it is to be known', and thus open to the charge of relativism. Nor is realism and a 'public world' as easy to avoid as is imagined by proponents of a starting point of 'my own private experiences'. 'If it is asserted', Anderson writes, 'that X is now experienced by me, then that is asserted as a fact, not as *my* fact, and as Moore indicated in "The Refutation of Idealism", it is a fact having distinguishable

---

[11] *Studies*, p. 32.

features – each of which, it may be added, is itself a fact.'[12] Like-wise, while, as is constantly mentioned by sense-data theorists, physiological and other conditions are necessary for perception to occur, it is quite erroneous (a further confusing of the -ing with the -ed) to maintain that, because my having a sensation of something depends on my nervous system, therefore *what* I sense depends on my nervous system, my mind, or whatever. The fundamental issue is one of the *ontological independence* of what is sensed. When I see, say, a cricket ball being hit, its being seen by me can be said, if we care to talk in that way, to depend on my having a sensory apparatus, being near a cricket field, the ball's having an easily discerned red colour, and so on. That, however, is merely to talk about the conditions on which my seeing it depends; the ball in no way depends on me for its exist-ence. But even where, as a further case, there is causal depen-dence, as when men build houses or bridges or manufacture cricket balls, there is still ontological independence: 'What exists because of me nonetheless *exists*, apart from or indepen-dently of me.'[13]

Anderson, of course, wants to deny that 'sensible objects' – the things that we ordinarily see, touch, etc., – are at all causally dependent on the perceiver's body for their existence, but what he argues can be applied to cases where there is causal depen-dence on the person, such as cases where someone has a green after-image of something, an ache in a wisdom tooth, and so on. (It is cases of this kind which some sense-data theorists seize on in order, with deep implausibility, to liken them to the plain man's *ordinary* perceptions.) But even cases of this kind, which involve complicated relationships in which the person's body and sensory apparatus have a vital part, are far from being instances of a simple datum, 'My experience'; what we have at least is 'My experience of X' where X is something complex and about which mistakes may be made and further questions asked – for example. What exact colour-changes does my after-image

---

[12] Review of S. Stebbing, 'Logical Positivism and Analysis', *A.J.P.P.*, 1937, p. 239.
[13] *Studies*, p. 33.

go through and what kind of configuration does it have? That is, despite the causal dependence on the person concerned of such items, or ingredients of such items, here too *what* the person is aware of, or believes he is aware of, is complex and ontologically separate from what it is in the person that is aware of them.

Anderson did not write at length on sense-data theories – nor did he follow up their twists and turns when they became very fashionable in the 1930's and afterwards; probably because he regarded them as merely perpetuating old fallacies – but he did, for example, endorse the standard criticism that, despite phenomenalist claims, statements about material objects cannot be successfully analysed into statements about sense-data, and he noted that the claim that they can has as little plausibility as the corresponding social atomist claim that statements about nations, social organisations, etc., can be analysed into statements about individuals. Moreover, although he was not, in general, sympathetic to Oxford 'linguistic' philosophy he could quite agree at least with J. L. Austin's view that descriptions of immediate perceptions are not incorrigible and that 'talk of deception only makes sense against a background of general non-deception'.[14]

Anderson did, however, go into some detail in reply to one characteristic doctrine of phenomenalism. This is the theory of 'looks' or 'appearances' as applied to pennies that look elliptical, objects that appear larger when they are close at hand, and so on, and according to which, for example, when a round penny appears elliptical it is supposed that the observer is apprehending an elliptical sense-datum. The fact of the matter, Anderson argues, is that if someone judges a round penny to be elliptical he is subject to a false belief and that is normally not the case. (Sense-data theorists are prone to exaggerate the occurrence of such errors.) We see things, including pennies, in *three dimensions* and under *complex* conditions. For example, we may see a penny against the background of a wall of a room, and if the penny is oblique it may conceal an elliptical part of the wall. In such a case we *need not* attribute to the penny the shape of its

[14] *Sense and Sensibilia*, Oxford University Press, Oxford, 1962, p. 11.

projection, but if, say, we fail to distinguish clearly between the
distances of the penny and the background wall we may suppose
that it is the penny which is elliptical. In such a case he comments:

There is something elliptical in the same direction as the penny, something moreover of which we only *see* the shape, and there is a consequent possibility of our attributing that shape to the seen penny. If,
however, something in the appearance of the object suggests that it is a
penny, then we doubt the supposition we have made, and by stricter
attention observe that the penny is not in the plane of the wall but is
oblique and round. The previous mistake may be described by saying
that we had 'displaced' the elliptical shape from the wall to the penny,
just as we might displace the red colour of red spectacles to the things
we saw through them.

Likewise, in other types of case, we *may* make mistakes but we
need not do so. For example:

We can judge sizes best when the things compared are close together;
but we *can* see a distant tree larger than a man near at hand, who, if he
stepped aside, would conceal the tree, and the relative sizes of the pro-
jections only appear to us in terms of concealed portions of a common
background. Improvement in discrimination is possible, and may come
about with the aid of other senses, as well as through the movements of
the observed things and of ourselves in observing them. But it could
never begin if we saw a flat picture.[15]

FALSE BELIEF

The general problem of 'error' or 'false belief', Anderson recognises, provides difficulties for any philosophical position, and in
realism's case the problem is to show how it is that we know
'independent real things' and yet can make mistakes about
them. He rejects, of course, facile solutions such as the one
offered by the New Realist, E. B. Holt, who argued that error
involves the existence of 'objective contradictions'; and he sees
also that phenomenalism itself (like idealism before it) cannot
really account for error: in the case of the penny, for example,
how, if I do have a sense-datum of something round and a sense-

[15] *Studies*, p. 36.

datum of something elliptical, can mistakes arise? As Anderson puts it, 'if a "false proposition" were simply a certain contemplated content, it would not be *false*; it would be a state of affairs that we found to occur'.[16]

His own view is that the type of analysis he gives in connection with the penny can be developed also in the case of other 'errors' of ordinary perception, such as the railway lines that appear to converge in the distance or the straight stick that has a refracted look in water, and more complicated cases of illusion and delusion such as that of the mirage in the desert or of an hallucinated man who introduces you to visitors who are not there. Anderson's general position is that what we apprehend is never simple and indubitably known – is not a 'whole nature' we 'know all about'; any supposed 'datum' or 'sensum' is a complex thing or, more accurately, a complex situation or state of affairs, about which we can make new discoveries and also make mistakes; and when mistakes do occur they involve the mind's *misplacing* of real ingredients of situations.

This, in logical language, brings us to Anderson's theory of the 'false proposition' – given that we understand that a proposition is what it is that we assert, truly or falsely, when we make significant statements. According to Anderson, when someone S believes that A is B and this is a true proposition, he recognises an actual situation, A's being B. That is, true propositions do not 'represent' or 'convey' situations, they *are* situations; though, to be clear, we should add a distinction Anderson did not explicitly make, namely, that the class of true propositions is not identical with the class of situations, for while all true propositions are situations, it is only the case that all situations are *potentially* true propositions; not all of them have in fact yet come to be believed or 'proposed' by somebody, and, in view of what Anderson calls 'the infinite complexity of things', not all of them ever will be.

But, given that true propositions are situations, *false* propositions, of course, are not; in the case where someone S believes a false proposition, X is Y, X's being Y is not a situation,

[16] *Studies*, p. 170.

though the terms or ingredients X and Y are real (are themselves situations).[17] There is, however a true proposition or situation involved: 'What is meant by the occurrence of a "false proposition" is explained by reference to the distinction of subject and predicate, as *someone's mistaking* X for Y (*taking* X to be Y when it is not).'[18] That is, S's mistaking X for Y is a three-way relationship between S, X and Y which arises from the fact that X and Y, as well as S, are complex or situational, and from S's seeking or demanding or unconsciously wishing for the occurrence of X as Y. The possibility of error (like the possibility of discovery) Anderson is thus emphasising, depends on the complexity of the items involved, including the complexity of mind, which is active and anticipatory and not a mere passive receiver or contemplator.

D. M. Armstrong has criticised Anderson's position of the 'false proposition' because, he claims, he gives an implausible asymmetrical account of true and false belief.[19] But Armstrong in his brief statement of Anderson's position (he does not quote him) ignores what Anderson has to say about complexity and about the activity of mind. It seems to me that, while there has to be some asymmetry in any account of the matter (in that the difference between truth and falsity cannot be entirely eliminated), there is still more of a parallel between true and false belief in the realist theory than Armstrong suggests. Thus, according to Anderson, there is in fact a parallel between the situations of true and false belief in that when someone S believes a true proposition, A is B, he takes A to be B, and when he believes a false proposition, X is Y, he takes X to be Y (compare Anderson's emphasis on the parallel between discovery and error). But there is, of course, the important difference in the two situations that A *is* B and X *is not* Y, and the further difference that

[17] That is, in standard relatively simple cases. In more complicated cases it may not be X and Y but *their* ingredients that are real – compare someone's genuinely believing, say, that 'Unicorns would do well in the Melbourne Cup' or that 'Little ghosts are afraid of big ghosts'.
[18] *Studies*, p. 170.
[19] *Belief, Truth and Knowledge*, Cambridge University Press, Cambridge, 1973, pp. 43–4.

when S believes A is B he may also recognise that he is believing
that A is B, whereas when S believes that X is Y this precludes
his recognising, at that time, the situation: S is mistaking X for
Y.

2

Rejection of rationalism
and relativism

The root of the trouble is rationalism – the attempt to find certain ultimates, certain identities from which a whole theoretical system will
flow.

If I say 'X is true for me', then I am saying that X's being true for me is
an absolute fact.

Anderson's realist view of the independence and objective
nature of situations, including ones that are known, is connected
closely with the topics dealt with in this chapter, his repudiation
of rationalism and its 'ultimates' and his upholding, as against
relativism, of the absolute or objective truth of propositions.

RATIONALISM AND EMPIRICISM

The dispute between rationalism and empiricism turned histori-
cally on whether there were 'higher truths', innate in the mind or
known *a priori*, or whether – as suggested by the development of
science from the seventeenth century onwards – knowledge was
concerned with matters of fact which had to be discovered by observation. Thus the rationalists advanced a conception of
rational knowledge consisting of indubitable or self-evident
truths, according to which – parallel for example to their conception of geometry – theorems or derivative truths are proved by
reference to primary propositions or principles that are themselves axiomatic or self-evident. So arose the doctrine of truths
of reason based on 'clear and distinct ideas' (Descartes) or on
'necessary propositions' (Leibniz) and which are sharply contrasted with mere empirical or contingent matters of fact known
by experience.

Now Anderson, as a thoroughgoing empiricist, rejects the whole rationalist conception of truths of reason and maintains instead that all knowledge involves observation of matters of fact – observation, incidentally, including introspection (that may be fallible) in the case of knowledge of our own minds. But what he stresses – as few other philosophers have done – is that the issue about ways of knowledge is actually a quite subsidiary issue in the conflict between rationalism and empiricism. Thus, 'empiricism', he writes,

has been connected, in the history of philosophy, with the view that there is only one way of knowing, and particularly that that way is what is called 'sense' in contrast to 'reason'; or, rather differently, that sense is the only *originator* of knowledge. But fundamentally the issue is logical; the dispute is about ways of being or truth, not about ways of knowing truths. It is only after it has been assumed that there are truths other than matters of fact, or that there are objects which 'transcend' existence, that a special faculty has to be invented to know them.[1]

For this reason Anderson takes it to be a merit of Greek philosophy, in contrast with modern philosophy starting with Descartes, that the Greeks concentrated on questions about being rather than knowledge and that when the latter question was raised, for example, by Socrates in connection with his distinction between 'thought' and 'sense' he made it plain that this was subordinate to his distinction between forms and particulars as orders of perfect and imperfect being respectively. Thus, starting with Thales, who held that water is the fundamental thing, Greek philosophers raised questions about 'reality'. In particular, the Pythagoreans were early atomists in holding that the real comprises certain mathematical units, numbers, and that everything else consists of certain arrangements of these units; Parmenides and Eleatics rejected the atomism of the Pythagoreans in favour of their own monism of the One; while Socrates[2] advanced as a compromise between their views a dualism of forms and particulars in which, however, the forms are 'ultimate' or more real than mere particulars. There was also, in

[1] *Studies*, pp. 3–4.
[2] As regards Plato and Socrates, Anderson followed the views of John Burnet.

Anderson's view, a realist among them; for he regards Heraclitus as having advanced a realistic, objectivist and pluralistic
view of philosophy. Similarly – so Anderson argues – while later
epistemology-oriented philosophers have made much about
questions of knowledge their systems or positions have basically
involved ontological distinctions, as is illustrated by Descartes's
dualism of substances or essences, his successor Spinoza's elevation of 'divine substance' to the status of being the one or ultimate form of reality, Berkeley's distinction between superior
'active' being and inferior 'passive' being, and the gradings of
truth and reality made by the Hegelian idealists by means of
their contrast between The Absolute and mere facts or
'appearances'.

Over the centuries in the history of philosophy – and the
history of error – it has mainly been a matter of monism, dualism
and atomism competing as the theories that were in vogue, and
in particular of an alternation by way of a tendency of dualism to
'collapse' into monism and of monism to 'explode' into dualism.
But in Anderson's view, when we are confronted by the
question, How many ultimate realities are there, one, two or
many?, the obvious and correct answer is *none*. That is, in opposition to all such overtly or covertly made ontological distinctions – or as Anderson prefers to say, logical distinctions – we
have to recognise the realist-empiricist position that there is a
single way of being or truth.

THE 'UNSPEAKABLE'

In his best known article on the subject ('Empiricism' 1927)
Anderson argues against rationalism in a distinctive and pithy
way, so I will first quote some key parts of what he says:

The chief, and I think final, objection to any theory of higher and
lower, or complete and incomplete, truth is that it is contrary to the
very nature and possibility of discourse; that it is 'unspeakable'...
Every statement that we make, every belief that we hold is a proposition. Since, then, the supposed higher and lower objects of experience both take the propositional form, we are concerned with a single

way of being; that, namely, which is conveyed when we say that a proposition is *true*. Deviation from this view must take the form of saying either that facts are propositional but ideal explanations are above the propositional form, or that explanations are propositional and what they have to explain are mere data, not yet propositionalised. But in order to indicate data or ideals, we have to make statements. If there were anything either above or below the proposition, it would be beyond speech and understanding. . . .

The objection to rationalism is just that what is meant by 'truth' is what is conveyed in the proposition by the copula 'is'. And logically there can be no alternative to 'being' and 'not being'; propositions can only be true or false. There is no question, therefore, of degrees or kinds of truth; of higher and lower orders of discourse, dealing, e.g., respectively with realities and appearances. The very theory that attempts to make such a distinction has to be put forward in the form common to all discourse, it has to lay claim to the 'being' signified by the copula, it has to face the direct question, 'Is it true?' Thus empiricism regards it as illogical to make such distinctions as that between existence and subsistence, or between the 'is' of identity, that of predication and that of membership of a class; and still more obviously illogical to say that there *is* something defective about 'is' itself.[3]

It will be seen that an evident core part of Anderson's argument here is his upholding of a single way of truth and being. He is pointing out that when we speak or think we have to assert or believe propositions, and that this kind of propositional objectivity is inescapable, even on the part of those who try to deny it; that is, that he who wants to assert a position or oppose a position has to do so by asserting that certain propositions are true. Accordingly, rationalist contrasts between higher and lower realities, ultimate explanations and mere facts, and so on, are 'unspeakable' or self-refuting because the proponent of such contrasts has to use discourse, has to assert propositions, in order to try to communicate his position, and in so doing he is forced to treat his higher truths, or whatever, as 'speakable' or propositional, that is, as involving ordinary, single level of being, things or situations.

But it should be noted that what Anderson is arguing has a close connection with his logic, including his *formal logic*. There is some indication of this in the quoted material on 'is', but he

---

[3] *Studies*, pp. 4–5.

does not develop the subject in the article in question. So while
the details of his formal logic will be set forth in a later chapter, it
will be helpful at this point to describe its general starting point.
In Anderson's view the logic of propositions—or the 'logical
forms' that there are—is something we all tacitly recognise when
we carry on discourse, but it can be articulated and confirmed by
reflecting on what it is to have an *issue of truth or falsity*. As he
argues (see for example *Studies*, pp. 137–139) when we strip
away the multifarious purposes people try to serve by what they
say and arrive at the real content or logical form, what we have is
the issue, 'Is it *so* or not?', which involves just one copula, the
objective 'is' of occurrence or of being the case. Rationalist
views are pre-eminently those which illogically try to *modify* or
qualify the copula by setting up various sorts or levels of 'is's',
but in order to be 'speakable' they themselves have to assume
the unambiguous single copula. Furthermore, although there is
only a single copula or level of being, we also find in the issue or
.proposition the following. (a) The distinction of *quality* ('are' or
'are not') between affirmative and negative propositions; (b) the
distinction of quantity ('all' or 'some') between universal and
particular propositions; and (c) the minimum two terms or sorts
of things it takes to have an issue – we have to ask of a thing X
whether it has a character Y, so that we have the distinction between the propositional *subject* and *predicate*. However, that is
only a difference of *function*; in any proposition the subject
'locates' and the predicate 'describes', but there are not two exclusive classes of entities – subjects and predicates or things and
characters; any subject can also be a predicate, any 'thing' is also
a 'character', and *vice versa*.

That is to say, contained in Anderson's criticism of the
'unspeakability' of rationalism is a vital interlocking theory of
propositions and situations: of the single copula and the single
level of being, of the complexity of propositional subjects and
predicates and the complexity of situations, and generally of the
logical features of propositions and the forms of situations –
which foreshadows, as well as the formal logic, his treatment of
the problem of universals and particulars, and his broad theory
of Space, Time and the categories.

The question of the logic has a bearing on our assessment of the efficacy of Anderson's argument about what is 'unspeakable'. He does employ that argument against a variety of views and his use of it has been criticised[4] on the ground that it is not sufficiently precise or worked out to be really effective against offending views. But to be clear – and fair to Anderson – there are two methods of approach that can be adopted here depending on whether or not primary emphasis is placed on his logic. Thus (1) we may start from the standpoint of not accepting the logic or at least setting it aside for the purposes of an initial statement of his position. In that case some of Anderson's particular arguments about what is 'unspeakable' may be more, and others less, acceptable. For example, his arguments defending the proposition and objectivity, and those defending a single way of being, may well be seen to have powerful force, at least by people who are not doctrinaire relativists or doctrinaire rationalists. Likewise, it may be recognised that Anderson is correct when, as mentioned above (p. 10), he criticises the idealist account of identity in difference because it involves asserting that A simultaneously *is* and *is not* B – and is thus a clear denial of the ordinary conditions of discourse. But there are other cases where his express appeal to discourse or speakability is less clear, as in his statement that when an 'opponent's view involves him in insoluble problems . . . this amounts to the same as contradicting the possibility of discourse',[5] or again when he says, for instance, that it is unspeakable to maintain that the mind is 'unitary', or that universals exist. However (2) we may adopt the standpoint, as Anderson did, of primary acceptance of his logic. In that case, the more dubious arguments may be seen to be clearcut, forcible ones – for example, the conception of a unitary, i.e. absolutely simple or non-complex mind, and the conception of a pure universal, = a pure predicate, will each be denials of the nature of propositions and their terms and so unspeakable.

In any case, Anderson does back up his general arguments by

---

[4] For example, J. L. Mackie, 'The Philosophy of John Anderson', *A.J.P.*, Vol. 40, 1962, pp. 280–2.

[5] *Studies*, p. 123.

more specific criticisms, as will be explained in what follows with reference to rationalism and to relativism. In the case of rationalism, such criticisms are readily available because of the fact that, as Anderson says, 'All theories of higher and lower realities are stated in terms of the common reality we all know – and, indeed, can be stated in no other way.'[6] As a good illustration he cites Locke's claim that matter 'supports' accidents, where the trouble is, as Berkeley pointed out, that we *do* understand how something ordinarily supports something else but we *don't* understand what it is to 'support' something in Locke's mysterious sense – though his use of the ordinary word may confuse us and make us think we do understand it.

DUALISM AND MONISM

The recipe for criticism Anderson is thus suggesting is that of scrutinising the terms and explanations used by rationalists for telltale indications that they do assume 'the common reality we all know', and he uses this recipe with notable effect in attacking various accounts of 'ultimates', including dualism and monism. In the case of dualism – a recurrent target for his criticism – he uses as a model the classic argument presented in the first part of Plato's dialogue, the *Parmenides*, where Parmenides is portrayed as criticising the Socratic theory of forms. According to that theory (which will be dealt with more fully later in connection with the question of universals) there are the two realms of forms and particulars with the latter being supposed to *participate* in the former. But as the argument discloses, whether participation is understood as *sharing in*, as Socrates says at first, or as *imitating* forms, difficulties emerge which prevent Socrates from explaining what the relation is. The problem is that whether the relation is participation or something else it has to be described as belonging to the sensible or empirical realm of particulars and so has the other term of the relation, forms. And this stands whatever *metaphors* Socrates draws on; he cannot

---

[6] *Studies*, p. 90.

help treating particulars and forms as joint items in the single situation 'This particular has relation R to that form'. As Anderson sums it up,

We all know what is meant by 'having a share of', as when the owl and panther were sharing a pie; we can see the partakers and the partaken of, and we can see the partaking going on. Similarly, when one thing 'comes under' another, or 'is copied from' another; we have often come across such complex, existing states of affairs. But none of these experiences helps us to understand the *real* 'participation'; it is something unspeakable.[7]

The general point that is illustrated here is that, in whatever way an 'ultimate' such as a form is said to explain or make 'really intelligible' ordinary things or facts, the explanation that is offered has to treat the ultimate and things or facts as commensurate, for example as each being able to enter into the relation of explaining and being explained that is being canvassed by the theory in question. But in that case the ultimate turns out to be a thing or a fact of the same ordinary, and ordinarily understood, kind as what is being explained. Of course, the stock reply to this is that it isn't fair to ask for an ordinary, empirical account of what the ultimate is and how it operates, because the rationalist is seeking to convey something new and to do so can only deal in metaphors and analogies. But that is dogmatic evasion of the point at issue unless there *are* literal concrete amplifications which can be given of what the rationalist is saying. For example, by way of contrast, when Freud was introducing his new psychoanalytic vocabulary – 'repression', 'fixation', 'displacement', and so on – he was able to give at least some concrete indication of the force of his concepts and explanations. But the rationalist, in failing to do this, is comparable to adherents of doctrines which pretend to give explanations by claiming that certain things are 'unknowable' or 'beyond human comprehension'. Until he gives some intelligible, specific account of what he is talking about his theory has no starting point; or put the other way round, as Anderson says, his speech

[7] *Studies*, p. 52.

'bewrayeth him': he has to utilise our recognition of actual or empirical things – he has to use words that we do understand – in order to seem to give content to the theory he is setting forth. That is why, as Anderson stresses, we are entitled to take the descriptions that the rationalist *does offer* seriously and empirically, and by examining them in detail to show that what he claims is not an explanation of, but an imposition on, the facts.

This is the basis for criticisms of the various other philosophical dualisms. Thus, in the case of the well-known divisions into the mental and the material, and the supernatural and the natural realms, what the critic concentrates on are revelatory references to 'interaction', 'points of contact', 'correspondence' and so on, for those ways of talking presuppose that both items in the dualism have comparable causal, spatial or other characteristics, that is, are both natural or empirical things. Again, to cite a criticism original, I think, to Anderson, according to Berkeley there is a division between active and passive being such that I, as an active mind, exist in knowing, and the table, as a passive idea, exists in being known. But this is vitiated by the fact that there are obvious cases that encompass both sides of the dualism; thus, the whole situation 'I see the table' cannot exist either in knowing or in being known – without, that is, our breaking down the dualism and recognising that that situation and its ingredients all have 'being' of the same single kind. Similarly, with regard to the related question of ways of knowing, Berkeley supposes that I know myself by way of 'notions' and sensible things by way of 'ideas', but in that case how do I know 'I see a table'? It cannot be said that I do so either by means of a notion or an idea without undermining the distinction and recognising that there is a single way of knowing involved.[8]

Anderson is likewise critical of monistic and atomistic views, because of their own retention of dualistic doctrines and for other reasons. Thus, in the case of monism (atomism will be discussed in the next chapter) we may have an unqualified version of that position, such as the one heroically presented by Parmenides when he contended that absolutely the only thing that is

_____
[8] Compare *Studies*, pp. 57–8.

real is the One. But this is another 'unspeakable' position, as is brought out in Plato's *Sophist* (244 b to d) when he points out that Parmenides, in order to expound his position has to assume that in addition to the One there exist further things such as the words 'one' and 'real' that are applied to it. Later monisms, in particular Hegelian idealism, have been 'more sophisticated' positions, but idealism too, Anderson argues, is unable to show how the One 'can have aspects at all, let alone the particular aspects it is said to have'.[9] In saying, for example, in his finished account of his position that the Absolute or One embraces, makes rational, its aspects, parts or diverse manifestations, the monist is assuming that the Absolute can be distinguished from its aspects, parts or manifestations. Similarly, when an idealist such as Bradley argues for the Absolute by criticising 'appearances', the trouble is that (despite his references to the criterion of 'rationality') the only standard or test he has is that of appearance: he has to start by employing premises which assume that there *are* differences, in everyday senses of difference, in order to set in motion arguments which have as their conclusions a denial of these differences – in other words, the conclusions are inconsistent with the premises. This is a type of criticism forcibly advanced by Moore and Russell when they pointed out that idealists regularly began by understanding references to 'parts' and 'wholes' in the ordinary way, for example, that a part is *not identical* with the whole of which it is a part, and yet, when it suited them, they tried also to maintain the *opposite* of this. Idealists, furthermore, face difficulties of dualism's kind when they set up gradings of reality by contrasting the reality of the Absolute with the inferior reality of other things such as its aspects. In describing the relationship, 'This aspect exists relatively to the Absolute', or in describing separately the nature of the Absolute and its dependent aspects, they are forced to treat the supposed different types of reality as being of the one, ordinary situational kind. For example, as Anderson puts it,

[9] *Studies*, p. 84.

when we say that the Absolute *is* self-subsistent and its aspects *are* relatively existent, we are recognizing the independent existence of 'the self-subsistence of the Absolute' and 'the relative existence of the aspects'; i.e., we are recognizing, in spite of ourselves, a single way of being.[10]

ABSOLUTE TRUTH

Discourse, as Anderson frequently points out or implies in making his criticisms of rationalism, proceeds by people putting forward propositions and as such is the vehicle for the communication of absolute or objective or literal truth, that is of truth. His basic defence of this position is that its denial is a patently obvious case of unspeakability as its deniers refute themselves by presupposing the very absolute truth they are seeking to deny. But, nevertheless, in this area, perhaps more than any other area of philosophy, the 'obvious' needs underlining and spelling out owing to the remarkably numerous ways in which, by mixing up the issue of absolute truth with other questions – such as questions about 'relative', 'partial', 'complete', 'conditioned', 'final', 'infallible' and 'relevant' truths (and falsehoods) – it is often held in educated as well as popular thought that there is no such thing as absolute or objective truth.

Anderson's defence of the obvious consequently takes the form of patiently pointing out how the question supposed to be at issue (absolute truth) is confused with other questions.

Appeal, for example, is made to verbal ambiguities in order to suggest that claims to truth are inherently vitiated by the existence of private understanding of meanings. But while ambiguities are certainly present in language and people do make mistakes about words, the reply to the relativist or anti-absolutist is that this does not often prevent understanding and the communication of literal truth from occurring. Thus, if someone misunderstands, say, the statement 'Anderson was a realist' by taking it to refer to an Anderson not intended by the speaker, we can correct this by saying 'John Anderson', and if

[10] *Studies*, p. 48.

necessary 'of Sydney University'. Again, in the case of contextual ambiguities that arise from using pronouns like 'I', 'you', 'he', 'she', it is quite misleading to argue, as relativists do, that here we have cases of 'relative truth' because, for example with 'He is in the room', the person referred to will not be in the room tomorrow. The point here is that the sentence 'He is in the room' can be used to convey many different propositions, but we need not confuse these propositions and we can quite clearly and objectively distinguish for instance between saying truly that 'X is in room Y at time t1' and saying falsely that 'X is in room Y at time t2'. Then, to mention just two other types of case that involve ambiguities, (1) there is the claim that we cannot even say that '2 + 2 = 4' is true because, when two drops of water are added to two drops of water we have *one* drop of water: which misconstrues arithmetical addition as a physical, effect-producing addition; and (2) examples of vagueness that are said to undermine objective truth, such as saying 'Portugal is rectangular': where there is certainly the possibility of misunderstanding but that need not prevent us from distinguishing between saying objectively but falsely that 'The borders of Portugal are the sides of a rectangle', and truly that 'The borders of Portugal are a rough approximation to a rectangle'.

That is, in these kinds of case there is a clear sense in which we do have 'absolute', 'eternal' or 'unconditioned' truth.

But that way of talking is again regularly equated by relativists with questions of *different kinds* about what is 'absolute', 'eternal' or 'unconditioned'. Anderson's rejection of rationalism does entail a rejection of 'absolute' or 'eternal' truths in the sense of ultimate or final truths, that is, of what is logically guaranteed or infallibly known to be true. There is, for instance, no 'absolute truth' if by that is meant 'ultimate' truth about the Absolute, no eternal or immutable truths about an unchanging reality, and no 'complete truth' in the sense of knowing *all* there is to know. As we have seen, there are no ultimates in Anderson's view and in line with Heraclitus he maintains that things are constantly changing, and also infinitely complex – so that there are always new truths to be discovered. Nevertheless,

there are absolute and eternal or unchanging truths; Socrates'
drinking the hemlock in 399 B.C., for example, having occurred
is such a truth; what the anti-absolutist has to claim to show, and
cannot, is that such a truth as this about Socrates will at some
time change into a falsehood.

Questions about 'unconditioned' truth and about the conditions of true belief are also potent sources of confusion in the
arguments of the relativist. We have in the first place, Anderson
points out, to take care to make the realist distinction between
the judger and what is judged, 'between the psychical conditions
of our thinking and the objective conditions of the occurrence of
which we are thinking'.[11] It is the former – involving our
interests and wishes – that leads us to *select* certain occurrences
to think about, but this does not mean that our so selecting
makes truth depend on us. There may, of course, be dispute
about whether a given belief – a given proposition we have selec-
ted – is true or false, or whether an 'alleged fact' is indeed a fact,
but the objective point is that 'if we now recognize that something previously alleged was in fact true, nothing has happened
to the fact'.[12] True propositions (including those dealing with
ourselves) do not depend for their truth on our believing them.

In the case of the conditions of facts or situations themselves,
the claim made by the relativist is that we cannot really arrive at
absolute truths because what we know is not 'unconditioned' but
subject to various conditions. This argument (which has affili-
ations with the rationalist view that in order to know something
we need to know 'all about it') depends on the fallacy of confusing the stating of a given situation with stating its conditions or
circumstances, that is, the other situations to which it is related.
As Anderson points out, if we cannot speak separately of particular situations but have to state their conditions, then a consistent procedure would force us to state the conditions of their
conditions, and so on for ever, when, of course, we can and do
avoid the infinite regress by speaking of conditions without

[11] *Studies*, p. 16.
[12] Review of the *Proceedings of the Sixth International Congress of Philosophy*,
     A.J.P.P., Vol 6, 1928, pp. 225–6.

speaking of their conditions, and likewise we can and do speak of the initial situations without speaking of their conditions. We can, that is, know and assert separate, individual truths.

Similar criticisms apply to the relativism of the idealists according to whom we cannot assert 'isolated' truths like 'A is B' but must bring in the Absolute by saying 'Reality is such that A is B'. But as Anderson points out, if 'A is B' means 'Reality is such that A is B' then that in turn means that 'Reality is such that Reality is such that A is B', and so on – when the fact is that if we can say 'Reality is such that A is B' then we can and do say simply 'A is B'.[13]

Underlying these various erroneous features of relativism is the fundamental criticism that that position is *unspeakable* for the specific reason that it is *self-refuting*, which, as Anderson notes, is a criticism that received its classic expression in Plato's *Theaetetus*.[14] Thus, the relativist refutes himself both when he puts forward his general theory of relative truth and when he makes particular applications of it. If he obligingly says 'It is true that there are no truths', that is, that 'The proposition "No propositions are true" is true', he obviously contradicts himself, but he equally does so when he says simply 'No propositions are true' for his assertion of that proposition manifestly presupposes that some propositions *are* true.[15] As this illustrates, intelligible discourse cannot help but raise objective issues of fact, cannot help but maintain that so and so *is* the case, and this applies equally to the relativist's own assertions. That is why also when he makes particular claims about truth such as that 'Verbal ambiguities make impossible the statement of objective truth', 'Propositions depend for their truth on being believed', or, in the case of the Marxian relativist, that, for instance, 'The beliefs of members of social classes are merely expressions of the interests of those classes', he is inadvertently, but *inescapably*,

[13] *Studies*, pp. 115–16.
[14] Compare John Passmore, *Philosophical Reasoning*, Duckworth, London, 1961, pp. 64–8.
[15] For a rigorous, formal development of this criticism, see J. L. Mackie, 'Self Refutation – A Formal Analysis', *The Philosophical Quarterly*, Vol. 14, 1964, pp. 193–203.

asserting as a matter of fact that ambiguities do *make imposs-ible*, propositions do *depend on*, and beliefs do *express*, such and such; he cannot, that is, 'get behind the proposition' or avoid raising objective issues.

3
Empiricism and pluralism

There is nothing in the least empirical in the conception of a 'distinct existence'. It is on the contrary the rationalist conception of 'essence' masquerading as a fact of experience.

The general conclusion is that all the objects of science, including minds and goods, are things occurring in space and time, and that we can study them because we come into spatial and temporal relations with them.

THE BRITISH EMPIRICISTS

As emerges from Anderson's criticism of rationalism, his empiricism is rather different to some other conceptions of 'empiricism' including that of the 'British Empiricists', Locke, Berkeley and Hume. Those philosophers were, in Anderson's view, empiricist to the extent of maintaining, as against the 'Continental Rationalists', Descartes, Spinoza and Leibniz, that important parts of knowledge are derived from observation, and in Hume's case in particular of criticising rationalist views of causation. But otherwise they are, like many twentieth century 'empiricists', in key parts of their philosophies open to the charge that they are *rationalistic* themselves.

Thus (1), Locke, Berkeley and Hume each has a view of ideas (perceptions, which include impressions and ideas, in Hume's vocabulary) according to which an idea is a mind-dependent existence or that whose nature it is to be known. That is, each of them makes important concessions to the Cartesian view of consciousness. For example, Anderson notes,

Hume, in spite of his criticism, later in the *Treatise*, of those philosophers 'who imagine we are intimately conscious of what we call our *self*', has assumed the *cogito* from the very beginning in speaking of the objects of our knowledge as 'perceptions of the human mind'; i.e., he

33

has assumed, like Berkeley, that they are known *as known* and thus as
relative to something else which is on a different footing.[1]

(2) These ideas or perceptions are assumed, in an atomistic way,
to be initially *simple* and *isolated*, or *pure particulars*; units, so to
speak, out of which more complex phenomena are constructed.
(3) With reference to knowledge, Locke and Hume, in particular, made undeniable concessions to rationalist views about the
contrast between rational and empirical knowledge in holding
that there was an important distinction between 'truths of
reason' and 'truths of fact' (Locke), or between 'relations of
ideas' and 'matters of fact' (Hume).

As we have seen in connection with Anderson's criticisms of
Descartes and Berkeley, he wants to repudiate the whole theory
of ideas and perceptions because of the conception of *dependent
existences* and consequent dualism that it entails. Furthermore,
he utterly rejects the associated view that ideas are primarily
simple and unconnected with one another. Given the assumption, he argues, of isolated or separate units (whether 'ideas', or
'sense-data' or other philosophical 'atoms') it is impossible to
account for connections or to derive continuity or complexity
from the postulated simple units.

These criticisms, directed here at the British Empiricists,
introduce us to two fundamental tenets of Anderson's overall
position, his view that everything is *complex* and his view of the
nature of *relations*.

COMPLEXITY

As part of his pluralism Anderson affirms 'the infinite complexity of things' and denies that there is anything absolutely simple,
anything less than a complex situation. He defends this position,
first, on the ground that *as a matter of fact* we never encounter
anything less than a complex situation and any analysis we can
make of a situation is always into further ingredients (further
situations) that are still complex. He does not deny, of course,

[1] *Studies*, pp. 106–7.

that in ordinary life we do distinguish between what we call the 'simple' and the 'complex', but maintains that as an obvious matter of fact any such 'simple' is only a comparative simple – what we call, say, a simple sentence, or a simple colour scheme, is not absolutely simple but merely simpler in compared respects than a complex sentence or a complex colour scheme. Secondly, he argues that, given the hypothesis that there are absolute simples, that hypothesis is unable to show how complexes can be derived from or reduced to them; which is not surprising since, thirdly, the hypothesis that there are simples – like the hypothesis that there is One – is 'unspeakable'.

For these criticisms, particularly the second and the third, Anderson draws on Plato's *Theaetetus* and *Sophist* (which, together with the *Parmenides*, he regarded as containing Plato's best philosophy). Thus, in the *Theaetetus* (201 d–206 b) there is an examination of a theory of elements and complexes that Socrates is supposed to have thought of in a dream. The theory is that things consist of simple elements and of complexes composed of these elements. The elements can be named but otherwise they are unknowable and indescribable – for to treat them as being describable would be to admit that they were complex. Complexes, however, can be known and described, for they consist of elements which by combining with one another, just as words can be combined to form sentences, provide us with objects of knowledge. This theory, Socrates goes on to show, is an untenable one. He takes the example of a syllable and its letters, and points out that the syllable may be regarded simply as the sum-total of the letters, or else as a single whole which is not merely a sum or collection of the letters. Applying these two possibilities to elements and complexes, on the first interpretation we could not know a complex without knowing its parts, but since the elements cannot be known or spoken of, neither could we know or speak of the complex – or, alternatively, if the complex can be known, equally the elements must be known. On the second interpretation, a complex becomes something which cannot be completely analysed into elements, and, therefore, if according to the theory what is unanalysable is unknowable, complexes as much as elements cannot be known. The burden of the criticism is thus that elements and complexes are equally unknowable and indescribable, or else equally knowable and describable but in the latter case the view that the elements are simple breaks down.

Now criticisms of this kind can be levelled against later views that seek to analyse and explain the complex by reference to the simple, such as the view put forward by Descartes in his *Regulae*, the views of the British Empiricists mentioned above and, in more recent times, the theory of logical atomism once sponsored by Russell. It is worth reinforcing the arguments of Plato – and Anderson – by noticing how they apply to Russell's theory.

Russell's philosophy of logical atomism[2] (which was an ontological accompaniment of his logic of material functions) starts from a theory of 'the structure of the world' which postulates a hierarchy of 'atomic facts' which are either 'monadic relations' (thing-quality facts), 'dyadic relations' (relations with two terms), or 'triadic relations' (relations with three terms), and so on. These facts are supposed to be ultimately composed of *simples*. The theory is thus similar to that put forward by Wittgenstein in the *Tractatus* according to which the world is a totality of independent atomic facts and these are composed of immediate combinations of objects which, in turn, are absolutely simple entities.[3]

Russell claims that we arrive at simples as the limits of analysis of atomic facts. Thus the terms of atomic facts are particulars (or individuals) which are denoted by logically proper names and are themselves simples. (He also takes universals to be or to consist of simples.) He does, however, complicate his account by making a distinction between logically proper names and ordi-

---

[2] Developed especially in 'The Philosophy of Logical Atomism', *The Monist*, 1918–1919; reprinted in his *Logic and Knowledge*, ed. R. C. Marsh, Allen and Unwin, London, 1956, pp. 175–281.

[3] Unlike Russell, however, Wittgenstein made no attempt to justify or give details about simples. Both of them later abandoned their theories, and in his *Philosophical Investigations* (pp. 21–2) Wittgenstein refers to the *Theaetetus* in criticising simples.

nary or 'relative' names and between logical particulars and 'relative' particulars. Thus, whereas 'this' and 'that' in statements like 'This is yellow' and 'This precedes that' denote logical particulars that are simple, 'Socrates' and 'Piccadilly', for instance, are only relative names and what they denote are series of classes of particulars. But despite this concession to complexity, he regards them as ultimately analysable into simples.

Now, in concordance with the *Theaetetus*, some very awkward questions can be asked about this theory – which is something that Russell himself, in his honest way, seems to have recognised, to judge from the variations in the account he gives of simples. Thus, on Russell's view, if simple particulars can be named but not known (as he does suggest in one place) then anything complex such as an atomic fact or an individual like Socrates (if regarded as not simple) will consist of a series of unknowable simples. But in this event we are in the untenable position that complexes cannot be known – if the constituent simples are unknown there will be nothing left of what they compose to be known. To maintain instead that complexes can be known is to admit that they are not composed of unknowable simples – so that the theory becomes otiose.

In order to avoid this conclusion, the alternative is to maintain that simples can be known, so that now no inconsistency arises from saying that in knowing complexes we are knowing a set of simples. But here a question arises about how many simples there are. If, as seems to be Russell's main suggestion, the set of simples is infinite in number, we can never know them all and, accordingly, can never know a complex which consists of them. Again, if to meet this it is argued that we can know complexes without having to know their simples (which Russell says in one statement is possibly the case) then this is once more an admission that complexes do not merely consist of simples, that, in fact, complexes are just as 'fundamental' or 'ultimate' as simples. And in this case, since the point of the postulation of simples is to give an explanation of complexes or facts in terms of something more 'ultimate', it is clear that simples cannot achieve this task, so that the assumed need for their introduction disappears.

But whether or not simples are said to be infinite in number, the decisive objection to this view that simples are known is that, because they are envisaged as *simples*, they would have to be unknowable – and indescribable or unspeakable. This criticism is that to speak *at all* about simples, to say they *are* simples, to try to distinguish *this* simple from *that* simple is already to treat them as complex things with various characters and relationships. Simples, that is to say, can only be unknowable and indescribable, though their proponents are then inconsistent when they say *anything whatever* about them, including trying to introduce a *theory* about them. This is the criticism, foreshadowing Anderson's account of the 'unspeakable', that is suggested in the *Theaetetus* and summed up in the *Sophist* when the Eleatic Stranger comments on the adherents of the theory of elements as follows:

In referring to anything they cannot help using the words 'being' and 'apart' and 'from the others' and 'by itself' and any number more. They cannot refrain from these expressions or from connecting them in their statements, and so need not wait for others to refute them; the foe is in their own household, as the saying goes, and, like that queer fellow Eurycles, they carry about with them wherever they go a voice in their own bellies to contradict them.[4]

HISTORY OF PHILOSOPHY

It is worth remarking that, as is suggested by the various references already made to Plato and the historical rationalists and empiricists, in Anderson's view the study of the history of philosophy is a very important way of learning about philosophy. As against many contemporary philosophers who eschew that study and proceed as if it is just a matter of making a 'fresh start' in thinking about philosophical issues, he stressed the analysis and criticism of past philosophers as a key method of

---

[4] Sophist, 252 c, translated by F. M. Cornford, Plato's *Theory of Knowledge*, Routledge and Kegan Paul, London, 1935, p. 258. Eurycles was a ventriloquist mentioned by Aristophanes.

recognising the problems and their solutions – for, more than most disciplines, philosophy is subject to social and psychological currents that make for retrogression as much as progress, so that very often the 'fresh start' philosophers are merely rediscovering or re-formulating the sound theories and arguments of past philosophers, or, or as well, repeating or compounding past errors and fallacies.

In the case of the British Empiricists, while Anderson criticises them en bloc for their conception of ideas as 'dependent existences' and for their tacit atomism, he does distinguish between them and between their contributions in philosophy. Thus, while he sees merit, for instance in Locke's attack on innate ideas, he takes it (as noted earlier) that Berkeley for all his overt idealism is correctly critical of Locke on certain issues, and furthermore that Berkeley was more empiricist than either Locke or Hume 'in taking the truths of mathematics to be as "matter of fact" as those of any other subject, taking them to be something that has to be *learned* just as anything else has'.[5] But it is Hume, of course, despite his own errors, that Anderson regards as making a very important contribution to the development of a realistic empiricism because of his work on relations, especially causality.[6]

HUME ON CAUSALITY

According to the then prevailing rationalist views, causality was either just a matter of creation, or a little more plausibly, of comprehension – that is, any effect B was already comprehended within a cause A because, for example, A had within it the power to produce B. Locke and Berkeley, as part of their empiricism, argued against the comprehension view that in fact cause and effect are distinct, but they also made certain concessions to the 'powers' view, and it was left to Hume to develop

[5] *Studies*, p. 163.
[6] A. J. Ayer (*Hume*, Oxford University Press, Oxford, 1980, p. 18) notes that N. Kemp Smith was the first commentator to treat Hume as an original thinker and not merely as 'an appendage to Locke and Berkeley' or 'a forerunner of Kant'. Anderson, in his teaching, took a similar view of Hume.

fully the criticism of rationalism on this issue. As Anderson sums
it up briefly, the treatment of causality, and of any other relation
as really a form of identity, 'was definitely exploded by Hume,
whose argument on causality is applicable to any other case. If
there were in A a "power to produce B", then B would be in A,
and no production would take place.'[7]

More fully, the argument Anderson endorses is that, granted
that there is a cause A and an effect B, to say with the rationalist
that there is in A a power to produce B is to say that by knowing
A we can already know its effect. (The alternative is to say that
the 'power' is the cause, but then, by parity of reasoning, that
power must have a power to produce B, and so on for ever.) But
manifestly this is not so; as Hume points out, apart from experience we might take anything to be the cause of anything else. If,
instead, we say that to know this power is not to know B – that it
is not *defined* as 'that which produces B' – then we shall have to
say that this power is simply a certain quality of A, say X, and
then the position will be that AX (the A which is X) produces B,
and we shall have to ask all over again how AX comes to have
the power to produce B. Hume's argument is thus that, if we are
not to have the effect comprehended within the cause to the
point of being identical with it, if the cause and effect are *different*, then we can attach no meaning to the conception of
power.[8]

Now, in Anderson's view, a positive account of causality has
to refer to our recognition of *whole situations* of the kind, A
gives rise to B, but unfortunately Hume's own positive view
relies on the notion of constant conjunction between discrete or
discontinuous impressions or ideas, so that he is no more able to
give a serious account of causality than he is of complexity of any
kind.

Hume's account of causality faces certain well-known problems a key one of which is a *circularity* that appears in his explanation of causal sequences. Thus his view, in brief, is that while
we do not experience an objective causal connection between A

---

[7] *Studies*, p. 45.   [8] Anderson Archive, *Lectures on Causality*.

and B (for example, between fire and burning) – we do not have an 'external impression' of this – there is a psychological connection. Since A and B have been found to be constantly conjoined in the past this produces in us the habit of expecting B when we have experienced A. The connection is in us, not between A and B; it 'is nothing but an internal impression of the mind, or a determination to carry our thoughts from one object to another'.[9] But the question then arises of *what is* this psychological determination that is supposed to replace objective connection, and the telling criticism that can be advanced is that if Hume were to make a serious attempt to account for this determination (he makes none) he would be forced to recognise objective causal situations.

Anderson sees the correctness of criticism of this kind[10] and also, of course, of the criticism that Hume, on his 'mental experience' assumptions should not be able to speak of a distinction between 'internal' and 'external' impressions at all. In Anderson's view, Hume cannot give a satisfactory account of the mental transition from A to B, any more than he can of what it is for them to be constantly conjoined, given his assumption that all we have before us are isolated, particular perceptions. So the solution – which brings us to Anderson's own theory of generality – is to reject Hume's assumption and recognise that we *observe in single situations*, the complex relationships A's giving rise to B (such as fire's giving rise to burning) or, in the case of mental transitions, A's passing into B (such as my noticing fire's passing into my thinking of burning). Given such single, complex situations, Anderson furthermore argues, it can be seen that *frequency*, as stressed by Hume on constant conjunction, has nothing to do with establishing the conception of A and B being related. That is, the question is not *under what conditions* we have come to associate A and B (which might involve frequency of their occurrence), the question is what it is we are

[9] *Treatise of Human Nature*, Book I, Part III, Section XIV.
[10] Compare N. Kemp Smith, *The Philosophy of David Hume*, Macmillan, London, 1941, p. 93; John Passmore, *Hume's Intentions*, Cambridge University Press, Cambridge, 1952, pp. 75–6 and J. L. Mackie's Critical Notice of Passmore's book, *A.J.P.*, Vol. 32, 1954, p. 62.

concerned with when we do notice A in relation to B. Here, once it is admitted that the whole complex can be known by a single act of thought (and otherwise there cannot be judgements such as that A causes B) it is implied that the complex can be known even if *repetition* has *not* taken place.

This, then, is Anderson's own positive account of generality, including causal generality, namely, that when we observe that something of the kind X is of the kind Y, or that it produces something of the kind Y, we are already, in single situations, acquainted with generality. But we may, of course, be mistaken – for Anderson, unlike rationalistic seekers after certainty, emphasises that the possibility of knowledge and discovery is always accompanied by the possibility of error, so that our apparent observations of generality are often mis-observations. That is, in the course of noting generality in various single instances, we may be concerned with a cluster of general propositions, some true and some false (some observed and some mis-observed), so that while we are correct in, say, taking all X's to be Y's we are also incorrect in taking all Y's to be Z's (as when a child in discriminating its first horse notices some general features of horses but also wrongly takes it, for instance, that all four-legged animals are horses). That is why, from a practical point of view, repetition of observations may be very important in enabling us to distinguish amongst the general connections we have observed/mis-observed – unfalsified and further confirmed ones we can continue to believe and the falsified ones we can discard. But the vital Andersonian point is that repetition of instances will not help us to move from a state of affairs in which we do not have any recognition of generality – do not have *a conception* of it – to a state of affairs in which we do. Given that classical view of the 'problem of induction', how to move from the non-general to the general, the problem is insoluble and Hume's scepticism on the subject is perfectly justified. But Hume's conception of the non-general is mistaken and – in line with situational realism – we can affirm that we do have general knowledge from the beginning of our observations.

Hume's problem about causality is a reflection of his problem about relations generally, which he himself sums up in a famous passage in which he speaks about the two principles he cannot reconcile, namely, that 'All our distinct perceptions are distinct existences, and the mind never perceives any real connection among distinct existences.'[11] That is, Hume sees that given the absolute distinctness of existences (the starting point of his own position) there is no possible way in which they can be related. But the solution of the problem, so Anderson argues, following William James,[12] is to recognise that Hume's view about 'distinct existences' is mistaken. Hume takes it that distinctions are obviously real but assumes that if A and B are distinct this is incompatible with A and B being connected, just as from a contrary point of view the idealists (in opposing views of the Humean kind) take it to be obvious that connections are real, but assume that if A and B are connected this is incompatible with their being distinct, so that the latter has to be explained away (by claiming that A and B are ultimately not distinct at all owing to their union with the Absolute). But against *each* of these views, the atomistic view of Hume and the monistic view of the idealists, there is no incompatibility between recognising both that 'A is distinct from B' and 'A is connected with B', as it is a fact about situations that we encounter both distinctions and connections, things as both distinct and connected, from the beginning of our observations.

In opposition to both atomism and monism Anderson is thus a *pluralist*, maintaining that there is an infinite number of infinitely complex situations each involving innumerable differences and relations. He takes the latter point to be an obvious fact of observation and something on which the occurrence of discourse depends, and he furthermore supports it by bringing out the difficulties of opposed positions. As outlined earlier, for example, *differences* are necessarily assumed by idealists in their own premises when they try to prove there is only unity or connection, and there are the difficulties about relations that con-

---

[11] *Treatise of Human Nature*, Appendix to Book I.
[12] Compare his *Principles of Psychology*, Macmillan, London, 1891, Vol. I, pp. 352–3.

front both Hume and the idealists. Thus, in Hume's case there is
his inability to account for manifest relational situations, though
this does not stop him on occasions (as in his deployment of what
he calls 'natural relations' in his theory of the association of
ideas) from inconsistently assuming that there are, after all, such
situations. Idealism, too, has difficulties over relations, some of
them the same in kind as those facing atomism. To show what
they are and to clarify Anderson's own account of relations and
their link with qualities, let me refer to Bradley's famous discussion of relations in *Appearance and Reality*.

QUALITIES AND RELATIONS

Bradley sets out to show that qualities and relations are 'unintelligible' and he does this as part of a programme of showing that
all ordinary facts are 'brute facts' or mere 'appearance' and only
have meaning when they are taken in the context of the Absolute or Whole. He first argues that qualities are unintelligible
taken with or without relations, and then goes on to repeat his
argument from the side of relations by arguing that they are
unintelligible whether or not they are taken with qualities. So,
concentrating on the second argument, we find he begins by
pointing out quite correctly that it is 'mere verbiage' to contend
we can have relations without terms. But, given that we have to
understand that it is two or more terms or qualities that stand in
relations, he then insists that how the relation can stand to the
qualities is unintelligible.

If it is nothing to the qualities, then they are not related at all. But if it is
to be something to them, then clearly we now shall require a *new* connecting relation . . . The links are united by a link and this bond of
union is a link which also has two ends; and these require each a fresh
link to connect them with the old. The problem is to find how the relation can stand to its qualities; and this problem is insoluble. If you
take the connection as a solid thing, you have got to show, and you
cannot show, how the other solids are joined to it. And, if you take it as
a kind of medium or unsubstantial atmosphere, it is a connection no
longer.[13]

[13] *Appearance and Reality*, Oxford University Press, Oxford, Ninth Impression,
1930, Chapter III, pp. 27–8.

Here he is presenting us with his famous dilemma on relations: given that A has relation R to B, either R is a nonentity or else we are led into a vicious infinite regress, for if R is to be 'something' to A and B, we shall have to have a new relation R2 to connect A and R, but then the question of the relation between A and R generates the same problem, if R2 is to be something to A and R we shall need a new relation R3, and so on at every step.

A key criticism we can make of Bradley's argument is of its underlying assumption of atomism in order to further the cause of monism. Bradley himself wants to reject atomism and does put forward some sound arguments – compare his own realistic criticism that the theory of separate ontological atoms cannot accommodate relations:

> If the relations are admitted to an existence somehow alongside of the reals, the sole reality of the reals is given up. The relations themselves have now become a second kind of real thing. But the connection between these new reals and the old ones, whether we deny it or affirm it, leads to insoluble problems.[14]

But in his own treatment of relations Bradley himself interprets them as if they were further terms – compare the telltale words he uses in setting up his dilemma, the contrast between 'solid things' and 'unsubstantial atmosphere' – and as a result, by making it appear that when A has R to B, R is a further 'solid' or 'real' along with A and B, he is naturally able to set going an attack which is indeed quite effective – but that is because the target for his attack is an atomistic view of relations. To take a concrete example (Bradley gives none in his chapter on relations), he is arguing that when, say, the book is on the table, either onness is a 'nonentity' or 'unsubstantial atmosphere' or else there must also be a further relation between the book and onness, and the table and onness, and so on through the infinite regress. But realists and pluralists, in their view of relations, are

_____

[14] Op. cit. p. 126n.

not adopting either a nonentity view or an atomistic view of relations. As James, Alexander and after them Anderson have
pointed out, a relation A has R to B, such as the book is on the
table, is a single, complex situation, or, as we may also signal its
character, it is a whole, continuous or integral situation. As
Alexander says, in the case of the relation of maternity, for
example, there is a genuine relation involved – the relation does
do its work of relating the terms – but it is not a separately existing thing in addition to the mother and the child, nor is the relation a quality of the child and the mother, any more than the
child is a quality or part of a quality of the mother.[15]

This position, that there are obviously relational situations
(like Susan is the mother of Sarah, Sarah is older than Sam) as
well as qualitative ones (like Susan is green-eyed, Sarah is tired)
and that it is a logical mistake to assimilate the former to the
latter, is at the core of Anderson's views on this subject, but
there are some associated issues that arise which can be indicated by mentioning a further line of argument advanced by
Bradley in defence of the view that relations are 'internal'. On
this occasion, though his argument is cryptic, Bradley does use
examples in maintaining that relations 'alter' or 'make a difference' to their terms; thus, in the case of the resemblance between two red-haired men, that fact is correlated with all the
other circumstances and characters of the two men, proper understanding of which brings in the Absolute, and the position is
the same, he argues, even in the case of spatial relations for
when, say, a man and a billiard ball change their relations each
of them is affected in their natures.[16]

Bradley's argument here is closely connected with the idealist
view that no part or aspect of 'appearance' can be considered in
abstraction from the Whole or Absolute, but if (in the light of
criticisms already made) we set aside that view, some questions
still remain that are raised by Bradley's contentions. Thus, William James attempted to reply to Bradley by agreeing that there

[15] 'On Relations: And in Particular The Cognitive Relation', *Mind*, 1912,
p. 310.
[16] Op. cit. pp. 517–20.

were some 'more intimate relations' into which the very nature
of the terms enter, as with the resemblance between the two red-
haired men, but also maintaining that other relations, such as spatial and temporal relations, are entirely external as they make
no difference at all to their terms.[17] But James's reply, the realist
can claim, concedes too much to Bradley in the one case by
making it appear that there really are 'internal' relations, and
too little in the other case by leaving himself open to Bradley's
charge, in the case of the man and the billiard ball, that if the
change of relation 'makes no difference' it is nothing at all. But
we can clear up the issue along the following lines. Resemblance, very often, as in the case of the red-haired men, is not an
ordinary relation but a relation based on qualities; it naturally
involves the intrinsic features of, for example, the red-haired
men because it depends on their having a *quality* in common.
However, in the case of other relations including spatial and
temporal relations, while they do not 'make a difference to' their
terms in a way that accords with the atomistic view of relations
mentioned above, it does appear that there is more to the situation than James makes out, and a way of bringing this out is by
asking, to put it very generally to begin with, whether the presence of a relation is correlated with one or other of the term's
having certain qualities (and certain other relations).

That there is such a correlation is plain enough in the case of
causal relations (for instance, George's chopping down a tree
alters the tree and tires George), but it also holds in cases of a
different type as with size being involved in George's being
taller than Henry, or, again, in a more complicated case like
George's loving Henrietta it is well-known that his loving her,
rather than someone else, may be dependent on certain characteristics that he has and she has. Moreover, as a different type of
case again, we can ask questions about the characteristics of
classes of things that enter into specified relations. Thus, obviously if A is husband of B, A is male and B female, but likewise,
for example, if A is an airline pilot, a racehorse trainer, a com-

---

[17] *Essays in Radical Empiricism*, pp. 109–10.

puter programmer, there are certain specific qualities attaching
to A in each case. Russell once made this point – with reference
to those relations which can change (for example, A is older
than B is an unchanging relation) – by suggesting that, given that
A has relation R to B, a change in the relation involves some
change in the proporties of A.[18] Ryle, in the same vein, developed a useful distinction[19] which I will adapt as follows. Given
that A has R to B we can have the views (1) that R is a necessary
condition of A and/or B having *at least one* of its qualities; (2)
that R is a necessary condition of A and B having *any* of their
other qualities (or relations). Now view (2) makes a sweeping
claim of the grandiose idealist kind that we can rightly reject.
But view (1) makes a much more modest claim about how relations do 'make a difference' to their terms which can be
applied to all relations including spatial and temporal ones.
Thus, in the case of a sheet of paper which is on and then off the
desk, just as the fading and other alterations in a sheet of paper
are affected differently depending on where it is over a period of
time, it will be likewise minutely affected over brief periods; and
similarly with the development of ever so minute flaws, changes
in the density, etc., of a billiard ball, there will be differences
depending on the exact positions of the ball.

If we thus agree with Bradley to this very limited extent we
have not, of course, made any concession to idealism on the central issue of internal or constitutive relations. The relations are
not *inherent* in the terms or *qualities* of the terms. Furthermore,
if when A has R to B, A has a certain quality Q, this is so as a
matter of fact and it requires separate empirical inquiry to find
out that it is so. That is, whether or not we know that a certain relation is correlated with a certain quality, depends on the state of
our knowledge; we cannot from knowledge of the relation *alone*
infer that A has Q, nor from the latter qualitative information
infer that A has R to B. This is what Anderson brings out in his
initial criticism of idealism for its confusion of qualitative issues

[18] 'The Basis of Realism', *Journal of Philosophy*, Vol. 8, 1911, pp. 158–61.
[19] 'Internal Relations', *Collected Essays*, Hutchinson and Co., London, 1971,
    Vol. II, pp. 85–100.

with relational ones, for example, confusing the qualities of the knower with the knowing relations he has to other things. 'The fact', Anderson writes, 'that we can in many cases come to a conclusion about X's character when we are told that it has a certain relation, is due . . . to our having the *additional* information that only things of that character have that relation' – as when we conclude that husbands are males or that knowers have minds.[20]

---

[20] *Studies*, p. 43.

4
Knowledge and mind

> Feeling gives us a basis for a general descriptive account of mind, that
> is, we can recognize 'affects' as real *qualities* of mental processes (or,
> what comes to the same thing as real mental processes), whatever re-
> lations, knowing, striving or other, they may have to other things.

I have indicated how, through examining the history of philosophy, Anderson comes to advance his own position. In this and
later chapters I proceed to elaborate specific parts of it.

Anderson's realist view of the knower and the known and
their relation, outlined in Chapter One, are developed by him
by means, in particular, of a criticism and expansion of the views
of Alexander. While he regarded Alexander's *Space, Time and
Deity* as a valuable pioneer realist work, he was also critical of
his philosophy for a number of reasons – including the unnecess-
ary concessions he made to idealism and his unabrasive
approach, as a result of which, as Anderson rightly suggests, the
realist impact of Alexander's work was much less than it might
have been, and his actual influence was as much in respect of his
*un*realist views, such as those concerning 'emergent qualities',
as it was in respect of realism. Consequently, Anderson himself,
in his teaching and writing, sought to repair Alexander's deficiencies and develop a thoroughgoing and uncompromising
realist position, and he did so in two main areas, those concerning mind and knowledge and (as we will see later) Space, Time
and the categories.

ALEXANDER ON KNOWLEDGE

Alexander, partly because of his interest in physiological psychology, came to advance a realist and indeed materialist view

of the nature of mind, maintaining that the mental is a complex quality of certain brain processes. As Anderson puts it in a succinct summary:

Professor Alexander emphasized the importance of the view that the categories applied to minds in exactly the same way as other things, so that a causal relation, for example, in which a mental process was involved either as cause or as effect, involved spatial replacement as well as temporal succession, just as in the case of 'physical' causation. In regard to the mind–body problem, in particular, Alexander rejected the doctrines of epiphenomenalism, interactionism and parallelism, and showed that if any relation was to be established between a mental and a non-mental event, they had to be connected in space. He concluded that mental processes occurred in the same place as certain cerebral processes and were in fact the very same processes – that mentality was a quality of certain events in the brain.[1]

However, in Anderson's view, Alexander also combined this promising position with certain survivals both of Cartesian and idealist conceptions. Thus it is *consciousness*, Alexander maintains, that is the *quality*, and the *only* quality of mental acts, and on the strength of this he denies – against Freud – that there are unconscious mental processes. Moreover, despite his often realistic view of relations, Alexander himself falls into relativism in his account of the relation of consciousness or awareness, as when he claims, for instance, that the two terms of the relation are (1) the act of mind or the awareness and (2) the object of which it is aware – to which Anderson rightly rejoins that this is like saying that the terms of the relation of paternity consists of *the father or the paternity* and the child. But this is a confusion of Alexander's that flows from another peculiarity of his position, his doctrine that minds have knowledge of themselves by means of what he calls 'enjoyment'.

The position [Anderson writes] was complicated by Alexander's theory of 'enjoyment', according to which a mental process could contemplate things below the mental level but could only 'enjoy' itself. This, together with the quite unrealistic assumption that the mind existed

---

[1] 'Mind and Knowledge – Samuel Alexander', *Honi Soit*, Journal of the Students' Representative Council, University of Sydney, 17 May 1939. As this short article appeared in an inaccessible magazine I quote it (here and below) in full.

only as a totality or 'ego', rendered it impossible for Alexander to explain how it was possible for us to make such an assertion as 'I see a horse', in which we implied that our relation to the horse was before our minds as a single situation, known by a single act of cognition, just as much as when we said 'The horse is beside the tree'. And the view that we were aware of processes in other minds by a third type of knowledge, 'assurance', merely added to the difficulties.

If Alexander had adhered to the implications of his Space-Time theory, he would not have made these distinctions, or his further distinctions between intuition, sensation and thought; he would have maintained, on the contrary, that the only possible kind of knowledge is acquaintance with situations in Space and Time, and that whatever knowledge of minds we possess is obtained by way of 'contemplation', that is, observation. He did, indeed, admit that beings at a higher level than ourselves ('angels') could contemplate our minds; but this emphasized, instead of removing, the difficulties inherent in the doctrine of 'enjoyment', which was a return to the Cartesian view of knowledge that realism was concerned to combat.[2]

Alexander, Anderson is pointing out here, has not emancipated himself from the assumptions that mind is a unitary thing and that, as is revealed by his views about contemplation and enjoyment, all consciousness is self-consciousness. In bringing out the difficulties of this conception of separated ways of knowing, which are similar to those (outlined earlier) that face Berkeley, Anderson is showing what is wrong with Alexander's position and at the same time is producing evidence in favour of his own positive view, which is that self-knowledge need not accompany other knowledge but that when we do have self-knowledge it is, though introspected, non-indubitable knowledge of the same logical kind as other knowledge. That is, awareness of other things and awareness of myself are awarenesses of the same commensurate kind, though when I am aware of something (including something in me) it is by no means the case that I must also be aware that I am aware of it; or put more precisely, in the case of my mental processes, if, say, mental process A observes the situation, *A horse is over there*, another mental process B may (or may not) observe the whole situation, *Mental process A is observing the situation, A horse is over there.*

[2] Ibid.

Furthermore, as Anderson mentions, the invention of a further way of knowing in the case of other minds, 'assurance' as Alexander calls it, only compounds the problem: given, for example, the situation, *I know that I am speaking to you about the horse over there*, this on Alexander's showing already involves three different sorts of knowledge, so that knowledge of this situation in turn would require the invention of a fourth way, and so on along the infinite regress run – which indicates, as Anderson argues, that in the case of other minds too our recognition that they exist involves a single way of knowing.

Another of Anderson's criticisms is levelled at Alexander's view that *compresence* or *togetherness* is the spatio-temporal relation that connects a mental process and what it knows. The difficulty here is that compresence is a symmetrical relation, so that when a mind A is compresent with B the converse also holds and we might as much say that B knows A as that A knows B – which is not what Alexander wants to maintain. The difficulty is the same, Anderson notes, as that arising with James's view that knowledge involves an intersection of knower and known (an intersection or confluence of sets of 'pure experiences' as James argues), for intersection is also a symmetrical relation. In giving his own solution to this problem, Anderson makes use of his previously mentioned conception of 'relations in an extended sense' and argues that a spatio-temporal relation like togetherness or intersection, while necessary, is not sufficient to account for the relation of knowing. This relation, being a relation in an extended sense, also involves the presence of a certain quality in one of the terms, that is, the knower needs to be a mental process and that is why the relation of knowing is not symmetrical. (It is, however, non-symmetrical, as distinct from asymmetrical, as one mental process may know another. Thus, when mental process A knows mental process B – and when it knows other things – the presence of the mental quality in A and its spatio-temporal relation to B is not all that is involved; when A knows B but B does not know A there is also the fact that A is active or directed at B whereas B, in this respect, is passive.)

MIND AS FEELING

But what is the quality, mentality, that belongs to mental processes and marks off the things that can know from those that cannot? That quality is not *consciousness* as Alexander mistakenly maintains and must be some specific empirical quality.

Anderson's own answer is that the specific quality is *feeling* or *emotion*. He advances this view by making an analysis of the traditional division of mind into three activities or processes, cognitive, conative and affective – or knowing, striving and feeling – which in the history of philosophy have either been regarded, as by the idealists, as complementary *aspects* of all mental processes, or else, as by Hume and his followers, as three *sets* of mental processes.

Anderson, in line with the findings of realism, criticises these traditional accounts. Thus the cognitionalist view is subject to the logical errors of relativism as it attempts to characterise mind by the relation of knowing, or being conscious of, and to suggest that there is such an entity as reason or intellect; and, at the same time, by assuming that 'consciousness' is the essence of mind, cognitionalists were unable to see the positive content of the Freudian conception of the 'unconscious'.

Similarly, he argues that conation is also a relation, though it has a very important role in mental life, as is brought out by Freud's theory of the *wish*, and recognition of this fact helps to reinforce the pluralist point that knowing is not an inseparable feature of mental processes. Moreover, given the complexity that, as Anderson stresses, attaches both to mind and to the things to which it is related, reference to conation enables us to develop a realist theory of *error*. For this theory (which was discussed earlier with reference to the false proposition – see pages 14–17 above) he draws on Alexander for its general basis and on Freud for the psychological details, and distinguishes psychologically between true belief – our striving or wishing for something and obtaining it – and error – our striving or wishing for something and, when we fail to obtain it, seeking unacknowl-

edged substitute satisfaction or release of tension. This is the
central distinction, but because of the existence in our minds of
numerous and conflicting emotions, tensions, overt and covert
wishes, etc., and because of the complexity of the things with
which we have transactions (they are not 'simple', 'mere data',
'infallibly known' etc.) there are various forms of error. If we
take true belief along with error we can distinguish a spectrum of
cases, ranging through hallucinations, illusions, self-deceptions,
confusions, to recognition of what is the case – or in Freudian
language cases varying between extreme dominance by the
pleasure (and fantasy) principle and that of dominance by the reality principle; though, in Anderson's (and Freud's) view, complete dominance by the latter principle is not a viable possibility
owing to the permanent struggle in any mind between objectivism and subjectivist illusions.

In connection with Freud, it may be remarked here that
Anderson is critical of Freud's work on certain counts, including
his tendency to treat a person's infantile characteristics and
struggles as *alone* determining his subsequent psychological
history when that history, Anderson argues, in fact involves a
pluralistic interaction of character and circumstances. He is also
critical of Freud's similar monistic treatment of the cultural factors in human life (including scientific and artistic factors) as determined by, and deriving their energy solely from, sexuality –
instead of recognising that such cultural factors are *independent*
(though interacting) factors in human life. But Anderson does
acknowledge the importance and basic soundness of much of
Freud's theory about the nature of sexuality: the unconscious,
dream interpretation, the aetiology of the neuroses and, as
noted above, about the role unadmitted or repressed interests
and wishes have in leading to the occurrence of error and fantasy. With regard to theory of mind it is Anderson's assessment
that, despite Freud's monistic tendencies, his work is of the
utmost importance in its insistence on determinism and objectivism in the mental field and on the existence of conflicting and
multifarious mental activities, that is, on the vital conception of
the *multiple*, as against the *unitary*, mind.

This endorsement of Freud's work, however, is with reference to his contribution to the science of psychology, as distinct from the psycho-therapeutic aspects of Freudianism. The former, Anderson argues, deals scientifically with what is the case, whereas questions about therapy and cure (for neuroses etc.) are further and subsequent questions about *policy* that have no necessary connection with the objective study of psychology. If, say, science tells us that Y gives rise to X and *if*, as a policy matter, someone wants to bring about X and is able to make Y come about, then he may intervene therapeutically and so bring about X. But there is nothing in psychoanalytic science that necessitates our in fact wanting to bring about X – as when, for example, X is supposed to be the Freudian conception of 'happiness'. Moreover, from an ethical point of view, our wanting X in such a case may be *opposed* to what is ethically good – which is something Anderson brings out, for instance, by asking the question (alluding to his own conception of good), 'Can "heroic values", can heroism and devotion, be reduced to, or at all accounted for in terms of, the pursit of happiness?'[3]

But returning to the question of the positive character of mind, it is with feeling – or emotions or 'affect' – Anderson argues that we come to genuine qualities of mental processes. It is emotions – such as anger, fear, pleasure, sorrow, curiosity – that characterise minds and enter into relations like knowing and striving with other things. These emotions have a general feeling quality in common but are qualitatively different from one another, and it is by reference to them that we can clear up relativist confusions and finally arrive at a positive, realistic and pluralistic view of mind. Anderson sums up this view in the following way.

The thoroughgoing rejection of cognitionalist doctrine involves the recognition of the following facts: (a) that a mental process may exist in us without our knowing it (as when we find out afterwards that we *were* angry or afraid); (b) that a mental process may exist without knowing (as in what are called 'nameless fears'); (c) that nothing mental is simple or passive, but that we have a vast complication of tendencies

[3] *Studies*, p. 342.

(tensions) which pass through one another, and become variously organized, in pursuits and aversions, strivings and capitulations, sentiments and interests of all descriptions; that 'intellectual pursuits' are thus operations of the *love of truth* (the inquiring spirit), developing from original scattered curiosities – for we have no reason to suppose that all curiosities are parts of one curiosity, all angers the work of a single faculty of Anger, etc. We thus have a conception of mind as a society or economy of impulses or activities of an emotional character.[4]

He argues that while emotions or feelings certainly *have* relations – we can be angry at, pleased with, various things, etc. – this is not to *be* a relation. He allows the possibility that feeling is a relation (so that the qualitative content of mind would be something not yet recognised), though he holds that in that case it would be impossible to distinguish feeling from conation. But he takes it that there is already much evidence that we do recognise feeling or emotion as the character or constitution of mind, even though it is true that this recognition is often only of a confused kind; because of the surviving influence of cognitionalism, and because, since we do not necessarily know what is going on in our minds (introspection is not infallible), many feelings lack names or are only named after their objects. Consequently, there is need for progress in psychology and in physiology.

MATERIALISM

Now Anderson's general position here is one of *materialism*. There are, of course, different meanings attached to that philosophical term and Anderson rejects the traditional rationalistic form of materialism according to which 'matter' or 'materiality' is the *primary* or *ultimate reality*. But, in rejecting psychophysical dualism, including its variants parallelism and epiphenomenalism, as well as the idealist view that everything is mental or spiritual, he holds that anything mental is a *material* sort of thing that is in *Space* as well as Time. His materialism, however, has to be distinguished from that of *behaviourism*, and from what in recent times has come to be called *central state*

---

[4] *Studies*, p. 74.

materialism or the view that the mind is *identical with* the brain.

   Behaviourism is the view that there is no such thing as mind or mental processes and that defensible statements about what is 'mental' really concern bodily behaviour or tendencies or dispositions to behave in certain ways. Now Anderson commends behaviourism for its emphasis on observation and its rejection of the notion of infallible introspection; but he himself argues, as we have seen, that introspection is a form of observation that is not cut off from but is connected with other forms of observation – we can, for example, observe situations like *I am afraid of X* where we have knowledge both of some of our mental qualities and of things outside ourselves. There are, he thus argues, real mental qualities that cannot be accounted for by mere descriptions of bodily behaviour; which is a view he also supports by reference to psychoanalysis:

Compare Stekel's view that nothing in the dream is true except the emotion. Dreams are one important ground of opposition to the behaviourist view that the difference, say, between anger and fear is just the difference between facing up and cowering or running away, that is, that there is no difference of emotional quality.[5]

   He furthermore objects to the 'logic' of dispositions or potentialities and argues that when human beings do genuinely have a capacity or disposition to act in certain ways, underlying them are certain concrete or actual characters. With everyday examples, like *Sugar is soluble* or *Glass is brittle*, the genuine inquirer will obviously not be content with a mere reference to 'potentialities' as in pseudo-explanations like 'The glass was broken because it was capable of being broken', but will look for underlying actual characters to be found in the concrete situations that are involved. In like vein he objects (as do other critics) to Ryle's dispositional account of mind on the ground that Ryle's dispositional or capacity statements require analysis, and when they are analysed we find they are elliptical or limited statements understanding of which requires us to recognise distinctive qualities in the persons possessing the dispositions or

[5] *Studies*, p. 75n.

capacities – or, in Anderson's terminology, Ryle also is involved in *relativism* as he fails to specify concretely what it is that has capacities etc., that is, what has certain relations to other things.[6]

The difference of Anderson's materialism from central state materialism is that he never regarded mental processes as *identical* with brain or neural processes. He follows Alexander on this point – though the latter, as we have seen, confusedly describes the mental quality as *consciousness* and further conjoins his view with a doubtful theory of *emergent* qualities. Anderson, in terms of his pluralistic conception of mind, insists that

any brain process differs from any other brain process and any mental process, if it is a brain process, will differ from other mental processes, from other brain processes, and from other processes of whatever kind – while at the same time there will be respects in which it does not differ from such other processes.[7]

That is, he takes the mental – like the neural – not just as a quality but as a thing-quality, or sort of thing, and of such a kind that it is a species of brain process (all mental are neural but some neural are not mental), just as human beings, for example, are a species of animal. Accordingly, his view of the mental as a spatio-temporal and material sort of thing is compatible with the view that mental processes may one day be observed non-introspectively, for example by neurologists.

Central state materialists, like Armstrong, maintain that there is an empirical or contingent identity (not a logical or linguistic one) between mind and brain; that is, that mental phenomena, despite apparent differences that point the other way, really are, as a matter of fact, cerebral phenomena – as, so central state materialists believe, is increasingly being confirmed by the work of neurologists and physiologists. Even here there might be some difficulty in distinguishing this view from Anderson's, especially when it takes the form of holding, not that the mental is identical with *anything* cerebral, but only with

[6] *A.J.P.* paper at Sydney University on Ryle's *The Concept of Mind*, 18 April 1956.
[7] *Studies*, p. 113.

certain kinds of cerebral phenomena yet to be specified precisely. But leaving that aside, a key point at issue between Anderson and central state materialism is whether physicochemical properties are sufficient to account for mental properties. As Armstrong puts it, 'A pure Materialist allows man nothing but physical, chemical and biological properties which, in all probability, he regards as reducible to physical properties only.'[8] Now Anderson would have undoubtedly regarded this kind of materialism as a too simple philosophical position owing to this reductionist claim – which is a type of claim he frequently criticised on the ground that it wrongly uses conceptions like complexity and arrangement in an attempt to account for genuine qualitative differences in non-qualitative terms. In Anderson's view, anything is material or physical in the sense that the findings of physics and chemistry apply to it. This is true of the material studied by biology, psychology and social or historical theory: but, nevertheless, there are features of the biological, psychological and social (distinctive categories to be delineated and regularities to be ascertained) that lie beyond the findings of physics and chemistry; and in the case of the mental, then, there are certain irreducible qualities which are not explained just by the physico-chemistry favoured by central state materialism.

Here we must distinguish between Anderson's general materialism and his specific empirical claims about what characterises mental phenomena. Thus, in criticising idealism, dualism, and so on, and arguing for a realistic theory of what is mental, he is setting out the general nature of such a theory – just as he does in the case of social science, ethics and aesthetics. In all these areas he first rejects certain rationalist and relativist confusions that hinder genuine study, and indicates in a general way – gives a *sketch plan* of – what it is to make an objective, realistic study of the subject concerned. Then he gives his own concrete answers to the key questions raised; in the case of the study of mind that *emotions* are positive qualities which are not identical with the activities of the brain, and likewise in the case of the other subjects mentioned, that what are central to them,

[8] *A Materialist Theory of Mind*, Routledge & Kegan Paul, London, 1968, p. 17.

respectively, are certain social complexes, certain good human activities, and certain aesthetically good characteristics of works of art. But if his sketch plans for these subjects are correct, they leave open questions about what exact empirical answers are to be given, and Anderson's own specific answers could still be mistaken. Accordingly, in the case of mind, while he believed scientific investigation will eventually confirm his view that what is mental is a qualitative species of brain processes, and probably that the quality is *emotion*, this is an empirical view that may be mistaken, and it is just possible that future research will show that the mental and the cerebral are empirically identical.

5
Universals and particulars

Realism must deny any sort of ultimate. In particular, it must deny 'universals', which is one of the points on which realism has hitherto failed.

There are no separate regions of the universal and the particular, but any situation exhibits both particularity and generality.

THE PROBLEM OF UNIVERSALS

The 'problem of universals', along with related problems about 'particulars', has been an abiding source of philosophical controversy, and one of Anderson's most original contributions to realist philosophy is the solution he offers to these problems.[1]

The problem of universals, put simply, arises when we ask what it is for particular things to have, or to appear to have, qualities in common and relations in common. We are constantly making statements of the form 'A is round', 'B is round', 'C is equal to D', 'E is equal to F', as a result of which it seems natural to say that the quality, round, belongs to different things and the relation, being equal to, to different sets of things, and if we wish we can speak specifically of these common characters by using the abstract words 'roundness' and 'equality'. There then arises the problem of how the *one* character can at the *one time* belong to different things or recur in different places, and the solution offered by many philosophers has been what is called a realist theory of universals (though one that differs markedly from Anderson's own realist treatment of the problem). According to this, abstract words such as 'roundness' and 'equality' name real universals which exist (or 'subsist') along with real particulars and it is the nature of universals to be

[1] D. M. Armstrong, who in his *Universals and Scientific Realism*, Cambridge University Press, Cambridge, 1978, gives an account of many types of theories, curiously dedicates the book to Anderson and yet does not discuss or even describe Anderson's theory on the subject.

entities that can be shared in by many particulars. Given this broad position, subordinate disputes then break out: such as about whether universals exist in a different realm (*ante res*) or *in* things (*in rebus*), whether there is a dualism of ways of knowing – 'perception' of particulars and 'intellectual apprehension' of universals – or about how, precisely, universals can be in 'many places at once'. But the fundamental contention is that there are universals and that there is an ontological contrast between them and particulars.

The main opposed view in the philosophical tradition is nominalism and related positions, which reject universals out of hand and offer a different account of what it is for things to appear to have characters in common. Thus, according to pure nominalism (maintained, for example, by William of Ockham and by Hobbes), all that things have in common are their names or the words used to describe them – so that, for instance, if A is round and B is round, all that is common to them is the word 'round' – but there is then a very obvious problem, that of trying to explain why things have *words* in common, so nominalist-minded philosophers have usually adopted some type of *resemblance* theory. According to this, we apply, for example, the word 'round' to different things because those things resemble one another; though, of course, to avoid inconsistency an attempt then has to be made to argue that such resemblances do not involve things having *characters in common*.

Now Anderson rejects both the view that there are special entities, universals, and also the nominalist view that there are 'pure' or 'bare' particulars. I shall here sketch enough of the historical discussions of the problem to make clear how Anderson criticises other positions and defends his own.

NOMINALIST VIEWS

Anderson's criticism of nominalist views will be dealt with fairly briefly as it is mainly directed at the conception of 'pure particulars' and has a close affinity with his already discussed criticism of *simples* and his endorsement of *complexity*.

Nominalists, says Anderson, are mistaken in principle when they rely merely on words or on resemblances: to recognise that things can have the same names and adjectives applied to them, or that they resemble one another, we must recognise that they share characters and indeed that each single thing in question *does have characters*. In the case, for example, of Berkeley's well-known criticism of Locke's theory of universals as abstract ideas (or of a theory Berkeley imputes to Locke) Anderson agrees with Berkeley that there is no such thing as a *general* or *abstract* idea because any character we think of will be some particular character, any idea of a man we form will be 'either of a white or a black or a tawny, a straight or a crooked, a tall or a low or a middle-sized man'.[2] But, Anderson argues – in line with his criticism of the conception of the absolutely simple – there are no pure or completely non-general particulars in the way Berkeley imagines. Thus, when Berkeley says our idea of man must be of a 'black' or a 'white' or a 'tawny' man, he is still using general words, and if we had to think of a man as something completely particular we could not think of him just being white, for there are variations amongst white things just as there are among men. To obtain his particulars Berkeley would need to specify exactly what purely particular shade of white was in question, and equally with other characters; which means that he could at best refer to them as 'this' or 'that'. But if (which Anderson denies) we could arrive at such unique particulars it would be a miraculous feat for them to stand for other unique particulars. 'To say that their simple nature was of a *non*-descriptive character would be to say that they were indescribable – and indistinguishable.'[3] In fact (as Berkeley tacitly assumes) there has to be a stopping point to the process of specifying particulars, and at any such point things are recognised and described as having general characters.

In the case of resemblance explanations of how we come to group things together and apply the same words to them, we may have the view, also advanced by Berkeley, and open to the

---

[2] *Principles of Human Knowledge*, Introduction, Section 10.
[3] *Studies*, p. 163.

objections just made, that bare or simple particulars can never-theless resemble one another in unspecifiable ways. Other re-semblance theorists, more sensibly, admit that compared things do resemble each other *in certain specifiable* respects. But in that case, Anderson argues, we have a recognition of complexity and of the fact that things do have characters in common. That is something which is substantiated indirectly by Russell's stan-dard criticism of the attempt to use resemblances to eliminate any reference to generality.[4] This is that in the case, say, of pairs of white things, A resembles B, C resembles D, and so on, we may ask whether these involve *common* resemblances or not. If they do, common characters have been admitted. But if there are *different* resemblances involved, either we set up an infinite regress of resemblances, or else we admit once more that the pairs of resemblances *do* have it in common that they resemble one another. But in that case, if resemblance can be common to things, there is no sound reason for not admitting that other characters can also be common to things. A further criticism of resemblance theories is that they start at *the wrong point*. That is, by making resemblance the primary issue they wrongly con-centrate (just as do theories that start with the question of *common* characters) on the *number* of things – two or more – that are involved and thus obscure what is the primary fact, namely, that things, singly, have characters.

REJECTION OF 'UNIVERSALS'

But if there are no 'pure particulars' there are no 'pure univer-sals' either – because there is no such thing as that which is just 'universal' and to try to talk about one of them is already to talk about '*a particular universal*'.[5] In confirmation of this blunt dis-missal of one of philosophy's prime metaphysical representa-tives, Anderson argues further that the theory that there are universals once more introduces an untenable ontological con-

---

[4] *The Problems of Philosophy*, Oxford University Press, Oxford, 1912, pp. 150–1.
[5] *Studies*, p. 116.

trast – between them and particulars – and is furthermore quite unable to solve the 'problem of universals' that it is introduced to solve.

Plato's *Parmenides*, which as we have seen (Chapter Three) is Anderson's *locus classicus* for criticism of rationalist divisions of reality, is also his source for the materials for a refutation of any theory that there are universals.[6]

The theory of forms, as attributed to Socrates by Plato,[7] is a theory mainly restricted to moral and mathematical notions – Socrates shrank for instance from saying there was a form of muddiness – but it suggests a general theory of universals according to which, when a particular thing A is X (is good, large, human, muddy, or whatever), there exists a universal X-ness in which the particular A shares or participates. The criticism in the *Parmenides* shows, especially by means of infinite regress arguments, that there is a fundamental contradiction in the supposition that there are forms. Thus, in brief, Socrates's critic in the dialogue, Parmenides, shows that in terms of the theory a coherent account cannot be given of what participation is. Each form, for example, is supposed to be simple and a unity, and so cannot be shared or participated in by many particulars without losing its unity – which leads Socrates to shift his ground and say that participation means, not that particulars share in forms, but that they are copies of them. Then there is the crucial difficulty generated by the fact that forms have been introduced to *explain* why things have the characters they have. When, for instance, we review two large things A and B this leads us to suppose that there is a single form, largeness, to which A and B are related and which explains their being large. But then, when we review A and B and the form largeness, we find that they too all have something in common (they must all at least be alike in being large) so that, by parity of reasoning, to explain this we

---

[6] Anderson, writing in 1929 and 1930 on the seriousness and soundness of these and other arguments in Plato's later dialogues, thus anticipated Ryle's independent assessment of them along similar lines in his articles on 'Plato's Parmenides', *Mind*, 1939, pp. 1–44, reprinted in his *Collected Essays*, Vol. 1.

[7] Anderson agreed with the interpretation of Burnet and Taylor that the Socratic dialogues of Plato largely reproduce the views of the historical Socrates.

should have a second form, largeness 2, in virtue of which A, B and largeness are alike, and then for the same reason a third form, and so on for ever – so that we can never explain what the forms were introduced to explain: why A and B are large.

The Parmenidean approach equips us to deal equally with other attempts to justify universals. First of all they face the problems of dualism. Either the relation of universals to particulars is left unspecified or is indicated only in metaphorical terms (in which case, as we saw earlier with 'participation' the relation has not been made intelligible and cannot be used as part of a theory), or else a definite, empirical relation is specified and it is revealed that the universals are themselves being treated as ordinary, empirical things. The same criticism, moreover, can be levelled at those modern theories which have adopted the evasive procedure of treating universals as 'lower' rather than 'higher' realities by relegating them to the status of *subsistent* entities, for that view, as Anderson says, poses the unanswerable question of how 'can we give any intelligible accounts of how a subsistent object can qualify as an existent one'.[8]

Secondly, the *Parmenides* shows why we need not – and cannot – postulate universals to give a positive account of what it is for us to have general knowledge. Thus, as is brought out in particular by the infinite regress arguments, to talk at all about forms and particulars, from the beginning each must 'be regarded as having characters of its own, if the one is to be related in any way to the other'.[9] That is why the appeal to universals cannot explain what it is for things to have characters in common; that is, to have characters. If A's having the character X is a problem that has to be explained by saying that A is related to X-ness, the very same problem breaks out about how it is related to X-ness, and there should be a second X-ness to account for this, and so on for ever. The attempt to stop short at the first explanation; that is, to accept without further question the relation of the particular A to the universal X-ness, shows

---

[8] Review of the *Proceedings of the Sixth International Congress of Philosophy*, *A.J.P.P.*, Vol. 6, 1928, p. 227.
[9] *Studies*, p. 51.

that there is a presupposed acceptance of the very kind of fact there is supposed to be a problem about, and on the same showing we can equally accept the first fact that things have characters. The outcome of the criticism, consequently, is not only that universals do not provide the explanation of a suggested problem, but that there is something logically mistaken about the problem itself. The problem in its various formulations: How can things have the characters they have?, What is the real reason for things having characters?, is mistaken because it presupposes that there is a genuine question requiring the introduction of universals for answer. Instead, we can simply accept the initial fact that things have characters; that is, that we recognise from the beginning of our observations are 'this-such' or 'particular-character' or more precisely 'particular-instance-of-a-certain-general-sort' situations. That is why, too, as Anderson emphasises, those approaches to universals which make the primary question that of why or how things can have *common* characters are on the wrong track:

We do not require to introduce repetition in order to understand a thing's being of a certain sort; a single proposition tells us that, and we have no occasion to think of 'sort' as a peculiar kind of 'recurrent' entity.[10]

THEORIES OF 'PURE' SUBJECTS AND PREDICATES

These criticisms can be reinforced by referring to two representative modern theories of universals, those of Stout and Russell – whose views also help to bring Anderson's into sharper relief because they each claim that there are two *exclusive* classes, things or logical subjects on the one hand and characters or logical predicates on the other hand, whereas a *rejection* of that claim is at the heart of Anderson's own position.

  G. F. Stout attempts an ingenious compromise between upholding the existence of universals and endorsing nominalism. Whilst other upholders of universals are united in assuming that particular things share in *general* characters, Stout main-

[10] *Studies*, p. 119.

tains instead that just as things are particular the characters they have are also *particular*.

'Of two billiard balls', Stout writes,

each has its own particular roundness separate and distinct from that of the other, just as the billiard balls themselves are distinct and separate ... What do we mean when we say ... that roundness is a character common to all billiard balls? I answer that the phrase 'common character' is elliptical. It really signifies a certain general kind or class of characters. To say that particular things share in the common character is to say that each of them has a character which is a particular instance of this kind or class of characters.[11]

These particular characters, he maintains, belong to the universal which he also calls a 'distributive unity'. This somewhat obscure concept is supposed to be a unity of instances, for example of the characters, round, which are taken to have a certain unity or connection in the manner, say, that Rhodes scholars or Olympic Games medal winners do even though they may be spread out all over the world.

Now Stout's theory may be said to make some advance on the theory of forms in that it gets over Socrates's problem about the unity of forms by allowing the universal, as a distributive unity, to be literally shared in by many particulars; but like the theory of forms it involves a vicious infinite regress. This arises from Stout's initial denial that there are common characters. Essentially he is saying that if A is X and B is X, the two X's are just as separate and particular as A and B, so that A and B do not have the same character X in common. Each of them, however, has a character which is an instance of the kind or universal X. But, as Ramsey argued,[12] if A and B cannot have in common the character X or any other character, they cannot have the common character of having instances of the kind X; they can only have instances of this character. They must, in short, have instances of having instances of the kind X, and so on *ad infinitum*. As a result the theory breaks down.

[11] 'The Nature of Universals and Propositions', in *Studies in Philosophy*, ed. J. N. Findlay, Oxford University Press, Oxford, 1966, p. 7.

[12] 'Universals and the "Method of Analysis"', *Proceedings of the Aristotelian Society*, Supplementary Vol. VI, 1926, p. 17. Ramsey was criticising a view, similar to Stout's, held by Joseph.

Stout admits, in effect, the force of this regress but offers the answer 'that qualities or relations belong to classes or kinds just because they are qualities and relations. Characters *as such* are instances of universals.'[13] That is, he provides for a stopping point at the second step in the regress; whereas two things cannot both have the same character, their characters do not themselves have to have further characters or instances in order to be of the same kind – they as such belong to kinds. His reply thus assumes an absolute distinction between 'things' and the 'characters' that are predicable of them, and will consequently fail if that distinction cannot be sustained.

However, in any case, Stout's reply does not save this theory from a vicious regress. This emerges when we ask what is the status of the relation – having an instance of – which he has introduced. Thus, his original claim that things cannot have common characters applies to relations as well as qualities; if, say, A is larger than B and C is larger than D, A and B cannot share with C and D the common relation being larger than; each must have a particular instance of this relation. But now suppose X is red and Y is square; each has a relation to a kind, that of having an instance of; but this relation cannot be common to the two pairs of terms; what we have are two instances of the relation, having an instance of. But what is the relation between them and that of which they are instances? It will have to be a further relation, having an instance of, Number Two; and so on for ever.[14] It follows that Stout's view contains a contradiction, to avoid which we have to reject his initial contention and recognise that there is no difference between things having characters and their being of general kinds.

Russell's theory, which he advanced in conjunction with his philosophy of logical atomism, is that there are two separate classes of entities, absolutely simple particulars, and universals – which also ultimately consist of simples (of a different kind).

---

[13] 'Are The Characteristics Of Particular Things Universal Or Particular?' *Proceedings of the Aristotelian Society*, Supplementary Vol. 3, 1923, p. 116.
[14] Compare Ryle, *Collected Papers*, Vol. I, pp. 9–10.

Simples, moreover, he takes to have their own special kind of reality. Consequently, in Anderson's view, Russell's theory is
vitiated from the start by these rationalistic assumptions, criticisms of which have already been described.

In addition, there is a further crucial part of the theory open to
forcible objection from an Andersonian point of view. This is
Russell's sharp separation of particulars and universals and his
view – which articulates clearly what is implied by the theory of
forms and many later theories, including Stout's – that there is a
corresponding sharp distinction between the logical subjects and
the logical predicates of propositions.

According to Russell, logical predicates require completion in
a way that subjects do not. Thus, while a subject like 'Socrates'
does not require completion, a predicate like 'red' is really a
propositional function of the form 'x is red' where x is some subject or other, and hence 'red' cannot be understood on its own –
it requires this completion. This distinction, Russell argues, is a
fundamental distinction; a quality or a relation term can never
occur except as a predicate; when it seems to occur as a subject
analysis will reveal that it is still logically a predicate. On this
basis he arrives at his distinction between the two classes of
entities, particulars and universals.

It is clear, however, that this distinction, requiring as it does
the view that statements about particulars do not require completion, depends on Russell's account of particulars as simple, as
things we can know apart from all their characters, and, accordingly, the objections already made (pages 37–8 above) to that
account apply equally to this view. Thus the obvious objection is
that if 'red' requires completion to be intelligible the same
applies to 'Socrates'. We are never concerned with anything
which is *just* Socrates but always with something complex which
is only recognised and spoken of as having certain characters.
Accordingly, the utterance 'Socrates' in complete isolation (as
distinct from 'isolation in context', such as occurring as an
answer to a question) equally does not make sense; we require a
complete statement in which something is said about Socrates.
In this case, if there is reason for saying that 'red' is really a

propositional function of the form 'x is red', where x is some subject or other, there is equal reason for saying that 'Socrates' also
is really a propositional function of the form 'Socrates is y',
where y is some predicate or other; and as a result this argument
for the supposed distinction breaks down.

It does not follow, however, that the distinction between subject and predicate in the proposition is merely a grammatical
distinction and has nothing to do with 'logical nature'.[15] It is true
that in an elastic language such as English it is possible to re-
express any subject–predicate statement in such a way that the
predicate becomes the subject. We can make use of abstract
nouns and express 'Socrates is wise' as 'Wisdom is a characteristic of Socrates', we can turn the active into the passive voice
and say 'Jill is liked by Jack' instead of 'Jack likes Jill', or again
we can use words with converse meanings and optionally say
'Sydney is south of Newcastle' or 'Newcastle is north of Sydney'.
Nevertheless, in all such cases a clear distinction persists. For
example, there is a great difference between saying on the one
hand 'Socrates is wise' or 'Wisdom is a characteristic of
Socrates', and saying on the other hand 'Wisdom is Socratic' or
'Socrates is a characteristic of wisdom'. In other words, the use
of alternative linguistic constructions does not eliminate the difference in the 'sense of direction' of the logical subject and the
logical predicate.

ANDERSON'S THEORY

What the above discussion discloses is that there is a genuine
distinction between the propositional subject and predicate but,
as against Russell, it is not an absolute distinction. Understanding the proposition to be a proposed or supposed situation or
occurrence (as distinct from the sentence or set of words used to
convey it), 'we can', as Anderson puts it, 'distinguish the functions of subject, predicate and copula: the subject is the region
within which the occurrence takes place, the predicate is the sort

---

[15] Ramsey argued this, in 'Universals', *Mind*, N.S. Vol. 34, 1925, pp. 401–17.

of occurrence it is, and the copula is its occurring'.[16] But while the function of the subject is thus to locate, and that of the predicate to characterise, there are no *pure subjects* or *pure predicates*; terms (that is, sorts of thing) that are subjects and predicates of certain propositions are, conversely, predicates and subjects of certain other propositions – which is demonstrated by the nature of syllogistic arguments: any syllogism has at least one term that occurs once as a subject and once as a predicate.

The opposed theory of exclusive subjects and predicates, Anderson argues, gains credence from the way in which philosophers, as well as people in ordinary life, tend to concentrate on *things* instead of facts or situations, and on *subjects* instead of complete propositions. There is, moreover, an associated tendency to regard linguistic distinctions, such as those between nouns and adjectives, as indicating absolute logical distinctions. But while names, pronouns, nouns and substantival phrases are commonly used to indicate things or subjects, and adjectives and adjectival phrases to indicate characters or predicates, these linguistic distinctions are a reflection of social and practical interests that human beings have. A proper name like 'Socrates' is usually used to indicate a subject but it can be used to indicate a predicate – we can well imagine one of Socrates' enemies saying, 'The man corrupting the youth in the market place is Socrates'.[17] As a matter of fact we apply proper names only to certain things, but we could easily give personal names to bottles, trees, etc., if we had sufficient interest in so doing; as it is we usually specify them by speaking of 'This bottle', 'That tree', etc., that is, by using demonstrative parts of speech which, depending on context as they do, usually indicate subjects, but nevertheless they do not specify *pure* subjects. To quote Anderson again,

It would certainly seem that expressions like 'this' are commonly applied only to subjects. But that is because they contain, besides a certain term, the sign of quantity which goes with the subject; the same

---

[16] *Studies*, p. 117.
[17] We recall that Anderson rejects the 'is' of identity.

term could be predicate, but it would not take the sign of quantity with it . . . Briefly, then, 'this' means 'the thing indicated', 'thing indicated' can be a predicate, and 'the' is a sign of quantity like 'all' and 'some', and is in fact equivalent to 'all'.[18]

In the case of nouns, it is a feature of language that some of them have corresponding adjectival forms – 'man' and 'human', 'rectangle' and 'rectangular', 'horse' and 'equine', etc. But many do not – as with 'bed', 'bottle', 'bridge', etc.; and likewise many adjectives have no corresponding ordinary noun forms (though they do have abstract noun forms) – 'yellow', 'round', 'sweet', etc. But again these linguistic variations can be explained on grounds other than logical ones.[19] Thus – in brief – while in the case of a term (sort of thing) like man, we have a very considerable interest in the two kinds of proposition, one where man is characterised and the other where man characterises, the same interests do not obtain in the case of terms which are conveyed only by nouns or only by adjectives. In the case of bed and bottle, for instance, our interest in propositions in which the term is a predicate is limited and adjectival ways of conveying these terms have not become established. On the other hand, in the case of adjective-conveyed terms, such as yellow or round, we have only a restricted interest in propositions of the type 'This yellow is A', 'That round is B', and still less occasion to assert plural universal propositions of the type 'All yellows are X', 'All rounds are Y', so that separate noun forms have not developed – or have done so only in special ways, as when we speak of 'The (Village) Green' or of 'Sweets'.

Anderson's position is that the positive content of traditional accounts of 'particulars' and 'universals' is that every situation exhibits both particularity and universality and that the distinction between these two complementary features of situations is the same as that displayed by the different functions of the subject and predicate in propositions. Grammatical and other

---

[18] *Studies*, p. 119.
[19] Anderson thus rejects the view (for example, of P. F. Strawson in *Individuals*) that there is any distinction in respect of particularity and universality, between 'sortal' terms like man and 'characterising' terms like yellow.

linguistic variations notwithstanding, there are no 'pure' subjects or predicates as any genuine term in a proposition is a
potential subject-predicate, that is, it is the subject of certain
propositions (including certain true propositions) and the predicate of certain other propositions (including true ones). This is
the logical language equivalent of saying, ontologically, that
there are not two separately existing items, *pure* things or particulars and *pure* characters or universals, all we have are
'location-descriptions' or 'thing-characters', that is, situations
which as part of their complexity are both particular and general.

6

Formal logic

What is of the first importance to the study of logic is the showing up of rationalist fallacies, the rejection of the primitive, the elementary and the certain, and the concentration on facts.

Formal validity is the only kind of validity.

Anderson, as we have seen, sometimes equates logic with what is more often called ontology or metaphysics, and his logic in this wider sense embraces such things as his account of realism, empiricism and pluralism. But when he comes to express this logic in formal terms as a theory of propositions, arguments and other logical relationships, he does so by developing it as a systematic, improved version of traditional formal logic.[1] That is, he largely ignores developments in modern logic because of his criticisms of that logic. These are, among other things, that modern logic departs from the rigorous traditional account of *form*; that the Russellian interpretation of the 'existential import' of propositions (that the terms of universal propositions may be 'unreal' terms) conflicts with realism; that the modern emphasis on tautologies and axioms is a continuation of rationalism; and that contentions such as that the propositional calculus supersedes traditional treatments beg the question because, for instance, the hypothetical syllogism and *modus ponens* rules of that calculus are merely arguments of classical syllogistic in disguise. As a result, he is at odds with the belief in the importance of modern logic and its approach to logical problems that is held by the majority of today's philosophers. While they may well admit the original and consistent way in which Anderson works out traditional logic, and while the realists and objectivists among them

---

[1] A concise statement of the connection between his general and formal logic is given by T. A. Rose, 'Anderson's Logic', *The Australian Highway*, 1958, pp. 57–60.

may be prepared to endorse his defence of a *single level* of situations and propositions and perhaps his account of particularity and universality, many will disagree sharply with the narrowness of his approach to formal logic.

However, without attempting to say any more about the complicated question of the character and details of the dispute between traditional and modern logic, I will go on to expound the various parts of Anderson's logic, allowing this exposition to disclose, at various points, why Anderson is so antipathetic to the bent of much modern logical theory. Then, at the end, I will raise some critical questions.

Logic, in Anderson's view, deals with the forms of propositions, which are disclosed by a careful examination of the nature of discourse. The forms of terms, propositions and logical relations are forms found in actual situations. And because his theory of situations is realist and empiricist, in his logic all terms are real and all propositions empirical. There are, moreover, negative situations as much as positive ones, and although there are no incompatible situations (no 'contradictions in things' as Hegel and some Marxists claim) the incompatibilities exhibited in discourse have an objective basis. Thus, for example, while there are innumerable situations of the forms *All a are b* and *No a are b*, there is no pair of situations with specific ingredients x_1 and x_2 such that *All x_1 are x_2* and *No x_1 are x_2*. Likewise, all the implications[2] of logic reside in facts about situations; for instance, whenever two situations of the forms *All a are b* and *All c are a* co-exist, a third situation of the form *All c are b* also exists.

FOUR FORMS

Anderson's logic is founded on the classical four forms of propositions, each of which has four constituents, quantity (universal

---

[2] Anderson's use of 'imply' or, meaning the same thing, 'formally imply' is quite different from Russell's use of 'imply' in speaking of 'material implication' and, differently, of 'formal implication'. Anderson rejects 'material implication' from his logic because, *inter alia*, it ignores the *connection* between antecedents and consequents and thus makes implication into something that is 'quite arbitrary or "magical" – divorced from inquiry', *Studies*, p. 145.

or particular), subject-term, quality (affirmative or negative copula), and a predicate-term. These are the *A, E, I, O* propositions: *All a are b, No a are b, Some a are b, Some a are not b*.

According to Lukasiewicz's now customary symbolism for expressing these forms the syllogistic functors *A, E, I* or *O* are written first, followed by the two terms which are symbolised by the lower case letters *a* and *b*, so that we have: *Aab, Eab, Iab, Oab*. (Anderson himself used the symbolism adopted by J. N. Keynes, according to which *XaY* stands for *All X are Y* and so on.)

As was noted earlier, by 'terms' are meant, not words or phrases, but actual ingredients of situations, actual sorts of things, and there are not two separate classes of terms, 'pure subjects' and 'pure predicates', as the distinction between the terms is a functional distinction within the proposition between locating and describing, and every term is capable of either function. Likewise, since situations have a single level of being, the copula is a *single copula*, that of predication, and it is illogical in logic (as elsewhere) to try to qualify the copula by setting up additional levels or types of copulae, such as the 'is' of identity, the 'is' of existence and the 'is' of membership of a class, or again the modal 'is's' of actuality, possibility and necessity.

LOGIC AND LANGUAGE

Ordinary language, as well as stating or purporting to state facts, makes use of a variety of rhetorical, stylistic, obfuscatory and other devices. But in Anderson's view the *logic* of discourse is a realistic logic of situations. Accordingly, ordinary statements and arguments usually need to be re-phrased so as to reveal clearly the *A, E, I, O* propositions and relationships that are involved. This process of expressing statements in classical *logical form* made up an important practical part of Anderson's elementary logic teaching and numerous able students, including those who became lawyers and judges, have testified to the impact this part of his teaching had on them.

Most of the re-phrasing that is needed is of an unexception-able kind, given the assumptions of classical logic. There are just two signs of quantity, *all* or *some*; the copula must be separately stated; terms must be genuine and expressed in independently understood words, and so on – so that for instance, *Many men mean well* becomes *Some men are well-meaning* and *The only books Evelyn Waugh admired were his own* becomes *All books admired by Evelyn Waugh are books written by Evelyn Waugh.* However, in the case of certain linguistic forms (such as hypo-thetical sentences) there are problems and these will be dis-cussed later.

NATURE OF TERMS

Every term and its 'logical opposite' are, as Anderson puts it, 'real terms'. Thus the terms *tree* and *non-tree* are logical op-posites because they 'exhaust the universe' (anything whatever is either a tree or else a non-tree) and there are things that are trees and also things that are non-trees. When an apparent term fails to meet this condition, that is, when either it or its logical opposite has no instances, it is not real and is not a term in prop-ositions. For example, *centaur* and *non-centaur* each fail to be terms, *centaur* because there are no things of this kind and *non-centaur* because it does not have a real opposite and is thus what I will call a 'universal term'; that is, it is true of anything what-ever. Similarly, for example, *existent* and *non-existent*, and *round square* and *non-(round square)* are only apparent terms. As Anderson expresses his condition for terms rather infor-mally, we may make use of P. F. Strawson's helpful conception of *presupposing*[3] and say that it is a condition of any prop-osition's being a proposition that it truly presupposes that both its subject and predicate have real instances and are non-universal terms. Consequently, putative propositions that do

---

[3] *Introduction to Logical Theory*, Methuen, London, 1952. Strawson, however, in his own interpretation of existential import, makes it merely a matter of the *subjects* of propositions being presupposed to exist.

not meet this condition do not qualify as propositions and have no place in logic.

Furthermore, with reference to singular terms, Anderson adopts the traditional view that singular propositions (ones that contain a singular term) are logically the same as plurally formulated propositions and are usually *A* or *E* propositions, though also, owing to the fact that there may be different phases or aspects of a thing in the course of its history, we can have singular *I* and *O* propositions. Thus, for example, *Socrates is a Greek* and *Socrates is sometimes ill* are to be understood and can be written, respectively, as *All Socratic beings are Greek* and *Some Socratic beings are ill*.

NATURE OF PROPOSITIONS

All propositions are empirical, or contingent. For in accordance with his thoroughgoing empiricism, Anderson holds that there is no genuine proposition the truth or falsity of which is established on *a priori* grounds, such as the form it has. This means that apparent propositions with the forms *Aaa, Eaa*, etc. (as used, for example, by Leibniz and Lukasiewicz) are excluded from the syllogistic system.

In the summary which follows of Anderson's rules of logic I will set out the details only in cases where those details are not given, or are given differently, in ordinary textbooks. For brevity, an arrow → is used to express implication, the equivalence sign ≡ to express two-way implication, and the ampersand & to express the conjunction of propositions. The term-opposites, *non-a* and *non-b*, are abbreviated to *na* and *nb*. In the case of complex terms, *both a and b* is symbolised by *kab* and *either a or b* by *vab*.

LOGIC OF TERMS

Terms, in addition to the integral place they have in the logic of propositions and their relationships, have certain special features of their own. Anderson brought to this branch of logic a rigour and objectivism that is usually lacking in traditional accounts of it.

(a) Extension and intension:

Every term, as part of its complexity, has both extension and intension. For example, *Socrates, poets, Australians* are all parts of the extension of the term *men,* and *rational, vertebrate, mammal* are parts of its intension. These involve objective characteristics of terms (and are not based on 'conventional' or 'subjective' beliefs that people happen to have). Thus the extension of a specific term x_1 consists of all the subjects of the complete set of true *A* propositions in which x_1 is a predicate, and its intension consists of all the predicates of the complete set of true *A* propositions in which x_1 is a subject.

(b) Extensive relations of terms (class relations):

e.g. the term *man* includes the term *poets.* There are five relations, established as follows: co-extension: *Aab & Aba; a* includes *b: Aba & Oab; b* includes *a: Aab & Oba;* exclusion: *Eab;* intersection: *Iab & Oab & Oba.*

(c) Intensive relations of terms:

There are five relations, established as follows. Co-intension: *Ananb & Anbna; a* intensively includes *b: Anbna & Onanb; b* intensively includes *a: Ananb & Onbna;* intensive exclusion: *Enanb;* intensive intersection: *Eab & Inanb.*

(d) Definition:

Anderson follows the classical theory of real definition of a species by genus and difference, though in accordance with his empiricism there are no 'essences' or 'essential properties' of terms. Moreover, what counts as a 'species' is any part of the extension of a term, and what counts as a 'genus', or as a possible 'difference', is any part of the intension of a term.

In Anderson's logic all terms, being real and complex, are in principle definable and in more than one way. A term *a* is defined by finding a genus *b* to which *a* belongs and a difference *c* which marks *a* off from the other species of *b*; that is, by establishing the propositions, *Aakbc* and *Akbca*. Anderson pointed out (what is rarely pointed out) that it is also necessary for the genus and difference to *intersect*, that is, it must be true that *Ibc*, *Obc* and *Ocb*. Furthermore, when a qualitative term is being defined it must be defined by a genus and difference, each of which is qualitative. In this connection Anderson often cited Plato's *Euthyphro* where the definition, 'Piety is what is loved by all the gods', is shown to be defective because a term taken to be qualitative is defined relationally. (The other traditional rules of definition, which state that a definition should not be metaphorical, obscure or circular, refer to term-words as distinct from terms.)

(e) Division:

A logical or real division divides a genus into species in accordance with a single principle. The species cited must exhaust the genus and exclude one another. Thus, if *a* is divided into *b, c* and *d*, it must be true that *Aavbcvd* and *Avbcvda* and that *Ebc*, *Ebd* and *Ecd*.

IMMEDIATE IMPLICATION

(a) Positive terms:

The condition that all terms must be real ensures that the classical rules for conversion and subaltern inference, such as that *Aab* → *Iba*, and *Aab* → *Iab*, obtain.

(b) Terms and opposites:

The key case of obversion (such as that *Aab* ≡ *Eanb*) is ensured by the requirement that terms must be non-universal. (If, for instance, unreal terms were still rejected but universal terms accepted, obversion would be vitiated; thus *All men are non-centaurs* would then be admissible but its obversion would illicitly commit us to an unreal term by yielding *No men are centaurs*.) Accordingly, the classical rules for obverses, partial contrapositives, contrapositives, obverted converses, and inverses, all hold.

RELATION OF OPPOSITION

The five relations of consistency and inconsistency that are illustrated by the traditional *square of opposition*, together with the further relations of equivalence and indifference (or independence), hold in their unqualified, traditional way – *Aab* and *Oab* are contradictories, *Iab* and *Oba* are in subcontrary relation, *Eab* and *Eba* are equivalent, and so on. Anderson, in his teaching, paid careful attention to these seven relations and to the conditions that establish them. For example, in the case of indifference (an illustration is *All politicians are liars* and *All liars are politicians* which, because they have the forms *Aab* and *Aba*, are indifferent) he emphasised that *four* conditions are necessary and sufficient to establish this relation, which are, given two propositions p and q, that (1) p's truth does not imply the truth of q, (2) p's truth does not imply the falsity of q, (3) p's falsity does not imply the truth of q, and (4) p's falsity does not imply the falsity of q. In the case of the other six relations, their conditions consist of sets of either two or three conditions.[4]

SYLLOGISMS AND SORITES

Modern symbolic logicians, because they do not require the terms of *A* and *E* propositions to be real, dismember the classical set of twenty-four valid forms of syllogism by rejecting nine forms with subaltern or strengthened moods. Thus, for example, *Barbari, All m are b, All a are m, therefore some a are*

---

[4] For a fuller discussion of this question, see A. J. Baker, 'Classical Logical Relations', *Notre Dame Journal of Formal Logic*, Vol. 18, 1977, pp. 164–8.

b, or, expressed as an implication rule, *Amb & Aam → Iab*, is rejected because the conclusion but not the second premise is taken to imply the existence of *a*. However, owing to Anderson's realistic treatment of all terms, the classical forms of the syllogism, and likewise of the sorites, all stand as valid mediate argument forms.

Anderson, it may be pointed out, has original things to say about the traditional theory of the *distribution* of terms. He elucidated that theory by his distinctive view of the extension of terms and noted that the rules of distribution, as applied to syllogisms, while helpful rules, do not explain validity but depend on the fact that certain syllogisms *are* valid.[5]

COMPLEX TERMS

As we have seen, in Anderson's view all terms are complex – as is illustrated by the fact that every term has both extension and intension – so there are no terms which are simple in the sense of lacking complexity. However, in his logic there is a distinction between 'complex terms', which are conjunctive or disjunctive terms (such as *round table, poets or musicians*), and ordinary 'simple terms'. Like Augustus de Morgan and J. N. Keynes (and unlike most writers on traditional logic) he emphasised the role of complex terms in logic.

Anderson, more so than his predecessors, was rigorous about realistic requirements as applied to complex terms. The logical opposite of *kab* is *vnanb*, and of *vab* is *knanb*, and in each case the terms (as with simple terms) must be both non-empty and non-universal. Thus, the term *white flower* satisfies this condition, but the apparent term *round square* does not. An important consequence is that, when there is any rule permitting the formation of a conjunctive or a disjunctive term, the replacement of proposition-forms by actual propositions is restricted to cases where a genuine term is formed. For instance, we can

---

[5] For a statement and development of this view, see Alice R. Walker, 'Observations on the Distribution and "Significance" of Terms in Propositions', *A.J.P.*, Vol. 38, 1960, pp. 120–36.

move from *All squares are rectangles* to *All large squares are rectangles* but not to *All round squares are rectangles*.

Complex propositions, i.e. propositions with a complex term, must also be empirical or contingent. This precludes such non-contingent forms as *Akaba, Akabknac, Aavab*. (But it may be noted that e.g. *Aakab, Oakab, Eavnanb*, are contingent forms.)

All the rules so far given apply straightforwardly to complex propositions, but in addition there are various rules of complex implication and opposition that arise. These are too numerous to be given in full,[6] but some key examples, especially concerning conjunctive terms, will be listed.

(a) Conjunctive terms:

(1) Addition and omission of conjuncts: e.g. *Aac* → *Akabc, Aakca* → *Aac*
(2) Addition of superfluous conjuncts: e.g. *Akaba* ≡ *Akabkac*
(3) Double addition: e.g. *Abc* → *Akabkac*
(4) Partial conversion: e.g. *Ekabc* ≡ *Ekacb*
(5) Partial obversion and transference: e.g. *Akabc* ≡ *Eakbnc*
$\qquad\qquad\qquad\qquad\qquad\qquad\qquad$ *Akabkac* ≡ *Akanckanb*

With the (5) form *Akabc* ≡ *Akanckanb* we move from a complex *A* proposition to what Anderson called its 'virtual contrapositive'. As will be explained later, he regarded this as of particular importance in verifying cause-effect relations in a given 'field'.

(6) Complex opposition: e.g. *Ekabc* and *Iakbc* are in contradictory relation, *Akabc* and *Oac* are in subcontrary relation.
(7) Mediate implication: e.g. *Aab* & *Aac* → *Aakbc, Aab* & *Iac* → *Iakbc*

Anderson, unlike most defenders of classical logic, did not regard the syllogism (and the sorites) as the sole form of mediate implication. He recognised that there are certain complex impli-

---

[6] For a description of a complete set of 71 rules for conjunctive terms, see A. J. Baker, 'Syllogistic with Complex Terms', *Notre Dame Journal of Formal Logic*, Vol. 13, 1972, pp. 69–87.

cations, such as the above, that are not reducible to syllogistic implications.

(b) Disjunctive terms:

Most rules concerning conjunctive terms have a complementary rule concerning disjunctive terms. Some illustrations are the following. Addition and omission of disjuncts: $Aac \rightarrow Aavbc$, $Avabc \rightarrow Aac$. Contrary relation: $Eavbc$ and Iac. Mediate implication: $Aac \, \& \, Abc \rightarrow Avabc$, $Aavbc \, \& \, Eab \rightarrow Aac$. There are also various mixed conjunctive and disjunctive forms, e.g. $Akanbc \equiv Aavbc$.

RELATIONAL PROPOSITIONS

Again unlike most defenders of traditional logic, Anderson did not play down the place of relations in logic. This flowed from his view of qualities *and* relations as two categorial aspects of all situations. Accordingly, relational propositions (i.e. propositions which contain relational terms) have the same ordinary logic as other propositions. These propositions are sometimes naturally expressed in the plural but many of them are singular relational propositions. Now, in Anderson's general view, singular propositions are formally *A, E, I* or *O* propositions, and to mark this they may be expressed in the plural. It thus does not matter whether we have plural relational propositions, e.g. *All rulers of countries are corrupted by power, Some descendants of philosophers are philosophers*, or singular ones, e.g. *Socrates sometimes walks barefoot on the snow = Some Socrates are walking barefoot on the snow*, or *Alexander the Great is a son of Philip = All Alexander the Greats are sons of Philip*; each of these propositions has a contradictory, an obverse, can figure in syllogisms, and so on.

There are, however, certain additional inferences that involve relations which, where they have a formal (as distinct from a merely material) basis, need to be incorporated into the system.

(a) Complex conception:

One such inference is what is traditionally called 'Immediate Inference by Complex Conception' – e.g. De Morgan's example, *All horses are animals, therefore All heads of horses are heads of animals*. If we use *R* to stand for *related in manner R to* this form of implication can be expressed as: $Aab \rightarrow ARaRb$. It is subject to the realistic requirement that *Ra* must be a real term.

(b) Transitive relational arguments:

In the case of relational arguments of the kind, *a is equal to b, b is equal to c, therefore a is equal to c, a is greater than b, b is greater than c, therefore a is greater than c*, a problem is raised for syllogistic logic. In Anderson's view logic deals with the forms of situations and as a result, as he says, 'formal validity' is 'the only kind of validity'.[7] Accordingly, since the above arguments and similar relational arguments are plainly sound, there is a need to give a *formal* account of them. His solution is to present a set of syllogistic arguments dependent on the fact that when and only when the cited propositions are true, there is a set of other propositions that are true. Thus, in the case of the 'equal to' argument, when *a is equal to b* it is true that *All measurable by a are measurable by b (=Amamb)* and *All measurable by b are measurable by a (= Ambma)*, and so on in the other cases. These further propositions do not give the meaning of the original propositions but they must be true if the original propositions are true, and they provide us with a formal basis for the given argument. This consists of *Barbara* syllogisms: *Ambmc & Amamb → Amamc* and *Ambma & Amcmb → Amcma*. In the case of the 'greater than' argument, *a is greater than b* if and only if it is true that *Ambma* and *Omamb* and so on. This gives us, as a formal basis for the argument; two syllogisms, one in *Barbara* and the other a choice of either *Baroco* or *Bocardo*. Taking *Bocardo*, we have: *Ambma & Amcmb → Amcma* and *Ombmc*

[7] *Studies*, p. 153.

& *Ambma* → *Omamc*. It is not difficult, he points out, to make a corresponding analysis of other cases. For instance, to know that *a is to the right of b* carries with it a recognition that *All things to the right of a are to the right of b* and *Some things to the right of b are not to the right of a* – so that we have a formal basis for all transitive relational arguments.

FURTHER ISSUES OF LOGIC AND LANGUAGE

(a) Identity statements:

Uninformative identities (e.g. *Aaa*) are not propositions, while informative identities are expressed by Anderson, not by a special 'is' of identity, but by co-extension of terms: *Aab* and *Aba*. Thus, the author of *Hamlet* is the author of *Othello* becomes *All authors of Hamlet are authors of Othello* and *All authors of Othello are authors of Hamlet*.

(b) Existence statements:

Similarly, there are no separate existence propositions. Statements such as *Tame tigers exist, Tame tigers do not exist*, are re-expressed in accordance with the principle that *ab's exist = Iab* and *ab's do not exist = Eab*. What then of statements of the simpler forms *a's exist, a's do not exist*? In these cases, what *a* conveys is an unanalysed or unarticulated proposition and we have to inquire into what, in the context of utterance, is an assumed analysis or definition that will yield an express proposition. Thus, in the case of *Dragons don't exist* one such proposition is *No reptiles are fire-breathing*, while in the case, say, of *Men exist* we may make use of the conventional definition and cite *Some animals are rational*.

(c) Hypotheticals:

In the case of hypotheticals Anderson sees, of course, that it is sentences of this type, in particular, which have inclined many philosophers to reject the four *A, E, I, O* forms as too exiguous. Anderson, however, argues that to treat 'if, then' forms as genuine *logical forms* is to subordinate logic to forms of human procedure. Hypotheticals do involve particular forms of speech that depend on interests and procedures, but these forms are only 'rough devices for dealing with matters that can be covered in an exact way by a categorical logic'.[8]

In defence of this view Anderson distinguished between three main types of hypotheticals. First, there are relations between terms, such as *if anything is a man it is mortal*, where what is logically conveyed by the form, *if anything is a it is b* is an *A* proposition, *Aab*. Secondly, there are relations between propositions, such as *If Socrates is a man then Socrates is mortal*, where what are logically conveyed are arguments. Thus, suppose we have the form, *if x is a then x is b*; we obtain a syllogism, *Aab & Axa → Axb*, when we supply the missing major premise *Aab*. Here the minor premise, *Axa*, is supposed by the speaker as distinct from being asserted, but, Anderson argues, there is no special logic of *supposals*; to take such a view is to subordinate logic to human procedures or attitudes. The objective, logical forms involved, whether they happen to be asserted, supposed to be true, or supposed to be false, are those of *A, E, I, O* propositions and their relations.

Thirdly, there are more complicated cases of relations between 'functions', such as *If the barometer is falling, then bad weather is coming*. Here there is normally a vagueness or inexactitude attached to what is said, so that careful analysis is needed to bring out the logic of the case, which is again that of presenting an *argument*. In particular, we need to find an unstated *field* to which the antecedent and consequent refer. Thus, in the case of the above example, Anderson cites *pressure-regions* as the field; that is, it is with reference to this field that a relationship between a falling barometer and bad weather is asserted. So with hypotheticals of this kind, e.g. of the form, *If a is b then c is d*, we need to specify the relevant field of *f*, and when we do so we obtain, parallel to hypotheticals of the second type, the syllo-

[8] *Studies*, p. 147.

gism: *All f such that a is b are f such that c is d, Here is an f such that a is b; therefore Here is an f such that c is d.*

(d) Imperatives:

Although he did not attempt to work out in detail his position in this area, Anderson advanced an analogous view about the logic of imperatives.[9] These sentences are commonly regarded as involving new or different *logical forms*, but in his view the evident differences of use between imperative and indicative sentences reflect merely *social* differences of procedure and interest. Imperatives occur in the presence of certain facts – e.g. *Stop smoking* when X is smoking and Y orders him to cease, that is, when Y seeks to bring about the situation *X is not smoking* – and their expression involves assertions of what is true or false. Similarly, conflicts of imperatives involve inconsistent assertions e.g. in the case of *Stop smoking: I will not* between *X is going to stop smoking* and *X is not going to stop smoking*. As such, so far as their *logic* is concerned, that is the ordinary logic of *A, E, I, O* propositions, though, Anderson is careful to note, imperatives are important sources of confusion about 'absolute necessity', especially in ethics (compare confusions about *categorical* imperatives or *absolute* obligations). That is, the use of imperatives may illogically conflate issues about what is true or false with issues about implication or logical necessity.[10]

SOME PROBLEMS

Anderson thus develops, in an original way, a rigorous, realistic account of classical logic. But certain difficulties still arise within that logic. Propositions with multiple quantification and cross reference cannot be handled with the same ease as in modern logic, and some practical (though Anderson argues not *logical*)

---

[9] Compare *Studies*, pp. 178–9.

[10] For a more fully developed account of imperatives as indicatives from the point of view of logic, see P. C. Gibbons, '"Imperatives and Indicatives", I and II,' *A.J.P.*, Vol. 38, 1960, pp. 107–19 and pp. 207–17.

disadvantages stem from the requirement that all terms be real. There may also be dispute, for example, about his account of singular propositions and of relational arguments.

Thus, with reference to his equation of singular propositions with ordinary *A, E, I* and *O* propositions, Anderson, in accordance with his view that all terms have generality, correctly treats singular terms as having phases or instances that make up parts of their extension, and so as being able to function as middle terms in syllogisms; and likewise he treats singular propositions as having all the relations of opposition, and so on. In other words, he correctly rejects the often voiced view that there is a sharp or absolute distinction between singular and other terms. But a problem is that his treatment of singular terms as having phases or instances invites us similarly to treat 'plural' terms like *men* as having, as well as their ordinary singular instances (Socrates, Plato, etc.), various phases of those instances, so that we can construct propositions like *All phases of all men are vertebrates, Some phases of all men are ill*, and so on, which show that plural terms have, so to speak, a double generality compared with singular terms. Moreover, we may argue that, just as in the case of all terms it has to be truly presupposed that they are real, in the case of singular terms there is the further condition that it must be truly presupposed that they are *single* things (for otherwise, in giving the logical form of, say, *Socrates is a Greek*, we should add *All Socratic beings are one* – but that is not something we really *assert* when we assert the original proposition). Consequently, it has to be acknowledged that, despite their affinities, there is a logical distinction between singular and other propositions.

Difficulties arise too in the case of Anderson's treatment of relational arguments because, it would seem, he would be forced to admit the existence of valid argument forms outside syllogistic. Thus, in the case of the 'equal to' argument, for example, for *a is equal to b* he substitutes *All measurable by a are measurable by b* and *All measurable by b are measurable by a*, and so on. But he recognises that the substituted propositions are not the same as, and do not explain the meaning of, *a is equal to b*, etc. It follows that, while the substituted syllogistic arguments are valid and obtain whenever the original argument obtains, the latter nevertheless also exists as an independent, non-syllogistic type of argument.

Another, wider problem, arises from the way in which Anderson relates his formal logic to ontology or general logic. He rightly sees that the account we give of forms of propositions and arguments will have to be connected with the account we give (or assume) of the nature of what is. In this respect he can be said to be in agreei..ent with the procedures of such philosophers as Bradley, who grounded his idealist logic on his ontology (maintaining that there is an ascent from singular to universal judgements and then to hypotheticals and disjunctives which are supposed most nearly to approach the concerns of the Absolute), and Russell, who related his truth functional logic to his logical atomist ontology (basing it on atomic facts the constituents of which are simple, or simples-containing, particulars and universals). For while Anderson repudiates their respective accounts of logic and ontology, he does wholeheartedly share with them the view that a defensible formal logic must be grounded in an ontology, his own being that of a single level of complex, spatio-temporal situations.

However, we may object that he has too narrow a conception of formal logic and logical theory when he identifies it with the study of 'the conditions of existence'.[11] Long ago, a group of us, as young 'Andersonians', used to spend much time discussing the question of 'the logic of situations' vis-à-vis that of 'the logic of discourse', and the distinction I believe has point. The former would yield a set of forms of implication but otherwise a very impoverished logic indeed, because, in a strict sense it would be concerned solely with the forms of *true* propositions and would exclude such things as contradictory, contrary and subcontrary opposition, counterfactuals and *reductio ad absurdum* arguments. All of these, it may rightly be contended, have as the basis for our understanding of them certain facts about the

---

[11] Compare, 'The Science of Logic', *A.J.P.P.*, Vol. 11, 1933, p. 314.

actual forms of situations, but the account we give of them nonetheless requires the introduction of the conception of falsity. But
once we have introduced the false proposition, we have something the analysis of which, as Anderson points out (compare
Chapter One), involves reference to a three way relationship
that holds between the terms of the false proposition and its believer or assertor. The fact, however, is that in dealing with
formal logic we ignore, as irrelevant, reference to the believer of
the false proposition. But, similarly, as Mackie has argued,[12]
hypotheticals, modals, and other subjects of modern logical
study, involve three – or more – way relationships and, as with
the false proposition, we can neglect the believer or supposer
element in the situation in going on to deal formally with these
subjects.

In the case of hypotheticals, for example, while Anderson
may be correct in bringing out their affinity with certain traditional forms, they are complex phenomena with special logical
features, including features that arise from something's being
merely supposed to be true or, in the case of counterfactuals,
being supposed to be false. Again, in the case, say, of the
question of real terms, formal logic as developed by Anderson
can be taken to be the logic of realistic discourse, but conjec-
tures or false beliefs about unreal terms (suppositions that certain true E propositions are false) do sometimes occur in
discourse, and it is open to us to take logical account of this; that
is, to extend formal logic by enlarging the place in it of false
propositions. Likewise, for instance, while Anderson is correct
in arguing that axiomatic or tautological forms, such as *Aaa* in
syllogistic or *p and q imply p* in the propositional calculus, are ar-
tificially derived forms that do not exist as forms of situations,
still, as a kind of branch of the logic of hypotheticals, by introducing these forms we can set out systematically various deduct-
ive consequences.

If these points are sound, Anderson can still argue, with
justice, that the forms of situations and propositions as he delin-

---

[12] 'The Philosophy of John Anderson', *A.J.P.*, Vol. 40, 1962, p. 278.

eates them are the basic materials for the study of logic, but the conclusion will stand that modern extensions and developments, instead of meriting blunt dismissal, have a genuine, though derivative, place in his formal logic.

7
Space, Time and the categories

When the separation [of Alexander's unrealist errors] is made, it will appear that in his doctrine of Space-Time he has laid the foundation of a thoroughgoing realism as a logic of events.

The whole point about categories, as contrasted with qualities, is that they apply to *all* material.

Most philosophical *systems* have involved rationalistic beliefs about the nature of ultimate reality; but in Anderson's view, given a realist and pluralist conception of a single level of reality and of the existence of an infinite number of infinitely complex situations, it is possible to have a realist system, or at least a systematic treatment of the general character and conditions of situations.

KANT AND ALEXANDER

Such a systematic, overall position is presented by Alexander in his *Space, Time and Deity* where, in what amounts to a rewriting of Kant's *Critique of Pure Reason* in a realistic way, he gives an objective, realist view of Space-Time and its accompanying categories as the pervasive feature of all occurrences or situations. Thus, with reference to Kant, while in Alexander's and Anderson's view he was important in developing a philosophy of things as spatio-temporal or historical, his system is defective because it treats what we know, namely what Kant calls 'phenomena' (= situations), as having several constituents or sources of supply: Space and Time, which come from mental *intuition*; the categories (notably causality) which are imposed by mental *understanding*; and the raw material of experience

95

which is derived from unknowable *things in themselves*, whose joint functions as conditions of knowledge Kant tries to justify by a complicated account of epistemological and psychological 'machinery'. This leaves Kant open to all the problems of onto-logical and epistemological dualism of the kind already noted and, as variant of trying to speak the unspeakable, to being in the position of *telling us*, as part of his theory, what is the nature of the 'unknowable'. But Alexander rejects Kant's theory of the conditions of *knowledge* in favour of a theory of the conditions of *existence*, according to which Space and Time are these con-ditions and we can also identify various pervasive categorial fea-tures of all situations – these situations and all their features and factors being *knowable* things as they are.

Now while Anderson, as noted earlier, acknowledges the con-tribution to realism made by Alexander's system, he was also critical of it on a number of counts and believed that it needed to be reconstructed into a thorough-going situational realism. Un-fortunately, however, Anderson did not complete a book he proposed to write on the subject of 'Space, Time and the Cat-egories', and we have to draw very largely on his teaching and unpublished writings. However, given that limitation, in what follows I will first summarise Anderson's criticisms of Alexan-der, and then set out, in some detail, the main points in his own position.[1]

In Anderson's view, Alexander's position is a mixture of rea-list and unrealist elements, both in connection with knowledge and mind as indicated earlier, and in connection with his account of what is. Thus, he objects to Alexander's *receptacle* or *substan-tialist* view of Space and Time and his tendency to regard them as a monistic *stuff* of which things are made (whereas Anderson treats Space and Time as the *medium* in which things occur). Furthermore, he criticises Alexander's treatment of the cate-gories as *predicates*; his conception of 'point-instants' as, in effect, ultimate units or atoms; his theory of separate universals; his conception of 'emergent' higher qualities culminating in 'Deity' which implicitly endorses the view that there is a series of

---

[1] This is based on the Anderson Archive Lectures on Alexander.

'levels of reality', and his general failure, as Anderson puts it, 'to have a logic' and to connect his overall position with such a logic.

SPACE AND TIME

Anderson's own account of Space, Time and the categories takes the form of giving a detailed account – a logical and onto-logical elaboration – of his view of propositions and situations as involving plurality and complexity. That is to say, he takes it that when we refer to Space and Time as the medium in which things are, to the connection and distinction between Space and Time, to the exact categorial features of situations, and to the distinc-tions amongst these categorial features, we are identifying and clarifying the variety of complex factors or ingredients that are, as matter of spatio-temporal fact, found in all situations.

His argument on the subject is very closely connected with his account of the form of the proposition. He insists that the only way to develop a defensible theory is by distinguishing consider-ations of the form as against the material of the proposition. In contrast Alexander, in failing to make that distinction and con-centrating on the question of materiality, was wrongly led to treat Space and Time as *things* or *terms*. But when we attend to the form of the proposition and expand on what is involved in the copula and the distinction between the propositional subject and predicate we can amplify our understanding of what it is for things to be in Space and Time. Thus, to say that things exist in Space and Time is equivalent to saying that things exist in prop-ositional or situational form which, specified further, is to say that what the copula conveys is existence in infinite Space and Time, while reference to the subject and predicate enables us to understand further the joint, but differing, roles of Space and Time as conditions of existence. In this connection Anderson argues that we can regard Space as the form of togetherness of things and Time as the form of their distinctness, so that it is as spatial that things can have location and be propositional subjects and as temporal that they can have distinction or peculiarity and be predicates; that is, that Space and Time have these different functions within Space-Time just as the subject and predicate have different functions occurring together in the proposition. Or, to make use of Alexander's striking metaphor, 'Time is the mind of Space', we can take this to bring out a parallel with body and mind according to which Space or body gives location and continuity to Time or mind, and Time or mind gives specifications and structure to Space or body, which is again comparable to the subject–predicate relationship of propositions or to the thing–character relationship of situations.

On the question of the complex nature of the Space-Time medium Anderson goes on to detail the correlation that holds between the three dimensions of Space and the three characters of Time. According to this, there is a correlation between one-dimensionality and successiveness in that successiveness in Time requires the existence of a distinct dimension or a possible direction in Space, and likewise there cannot be a direction in Space without there being a successiveness in Time. Then the second character of Time, its transitiveness and the difference of direction of a relation it involves, is correlated with the two-dimensionality of difference of direction in Space (as in an angle). While the third character of Time, irreversibility or absolute difference of temporal direction is correlated with three-dimensionality or absolute difference of spatial direction. (Anderson criticises Alexander for wrongly correlating the third character of Time with two-dimensionality and its second character with three-dimensionality.) There is no question here of presenting some 'ultimate explanation' of Space or Time, but it is a fact that each has three independent features and it is their correlation, in the way indicated, which discloses how Space and Time coalesce, or work together as Space-Time.

DEDUCTION OF THE CATEGORIES

Having connected his account of Space and Time with the form of the proposition, Anderson goes on likewise to argue that what are further involved in being or spatio-temporality, the categories, are also involved in *being propositional*. Consequently, he proceeds to present a 'deduction' of the categories which has an affinity with the procedure adopted by Kant in what is known as his 'Metaphysical Deduction of the Categories' when he connected his categories with forms of judgement (for example, the categories of unity, plurality and totality with universal, particular and singular judgements). However, Anderson's categories and propositional forms are not identical with those of Kant.

Group one:

Thus, starting with the category of identity, Anderson regards this as being occupation of a Space-Time, and so as being a subject of a proposition; for when we identify a thing by locating it we are, in the language of logic, finding out what subject it is. But such a subject is never a pure subject; it is something complex and points the way to further categories. This is brought out, first of all, by the fact that the subject is not a whole proposition, which introduces the category of difference – that is, the fact that situations have difference as well as identity. Then, by reference to the copula of the proposition, we recognise the category of existence (or occurrence or actuality); while the distinction between the affirmative and negative copula introduces the notion of coupling or relating things and of different ways of doing so, which brings us to the category of relation. Then this initial analysis of the form of the proposition is completed by the introduction of the other term, the predicate, to which the subject is related, which gives us the category of quality or universality, the indication of which is pre-eminently the function of the logical predicate.

Now all the categories are present everywhere – all are involved in all situations or propositions – but Anderson's argument is that we can discriminate amongst them and, by noting the particular connections they have with the proposition and with one another, arrive at the above categories. These, identity, difference, existence, relation and universality, are the initial group of what Anderson sometimes calls the 'situational or propositional categories' (though he varies in his views on what

are the best names for these and the other groups). But they are
not the only categories, as when we make further specifications
of the nature of situations, or – what amounts to the same –
when we make explicit further connections and distinctions
involved in the initial deductions, we arrive in all at a grouping
of three sets of categories.

Group two:

If we start with universality, the last category of the first group,
and consider it now from the point of view of being a subject (for
the distinction between subjects and predicates is only a functional distinction) then because, in Anderson's view, all
measurement involves *universality* or *kind*, we can go on to
deduce a set of categories concerned with mathematics or quantity.

It is a central part of Anderson's position, as we saw in Chapter
Five, that particularity and universality are inseparable, complementary features of all situations, so given universality as the
first category in the new group we can move on to the category
of particularity (which thus corresponds to the category of difference in the first group). As this category involves the instan-
tiation of kinds or qualities it leads on to the notion of the
membership of *classes*, which brings us in turn to *number* and
other mathematical categories. The key passage here from kinds
to classes arises because, in Anderson's view, our recognition of
classes and their members and our further recognition of their
numerical properties (that we have a pair of so and so, a quartet
of such and such, or whatever) depends on our recognising that
they are *alike* in certain respects. We come to recognise, say,
that A, B, and C are members of a class only because we have, if
only vaguely, taken it that there is some quality X they have in
common. Expressed formally, we take it that *All A are X, All B
are X* and *All C are X* and from this derive (by a complex term
form of inference) *All A or B or C are X*, that is, we form the
class-membership disjunctive term A *or B or C*, and may go on,
for example, and find out numerical facts about it.

Anderson maintains (in agreement with what Russell argues

in his early work, *The Principles of Mathematics*) that considerations of number begin with integers. These, in his view, are
characteristics of sets of members of classes with which we are
observationally acquainted when we learn to count. But while
we are thus concerned with integers to begin with, he denies that
there is any sharp separation of numbers as discrete units from
questions about continuity – and he expressly rejects attempts,
such as those made by Pythagoreans, to derive continuity from
supposed absolute units. On the contrary, he argues, there is no
such thing as an absolute unit – in the case of numbers there is
nothing which is just *one, two*, etc., but always *one person, two
apples*, or whatever. Nor is there any absolute number which
attaches to any given thing or situation: owing to the complexity
of things, including the number of ways in which they can be
counted, a given thing or situation may be one in respect of X,
ten in respect of Y, none in respect of Z, and so on.

Accordingly, there is a natural transition from the category of
number, which is specially concerned with integers or cardinal
number, to the other mathematical categories. Given number,
by a further step which involves introducing the conception of
asymmetrical or irreversible relations, we move to the category
of order, which includes ordinal number. Then, consideration of
subsequent mathematical questions – concerning fractions, real
number, etc., – leads us to the category of quantity, which is that
which goes beyond measurement by discrete units and is concerned especially with the spatial extension of things rather than
especially with things being of kinds or having qualities.

Anderson's account of these categories has a close relation to
his treatment of mathematics as an observational science (which
has been mentioned in connection with his empiricism but not
yet explained). As against rationalist views of mathematics –
such as that the subject rests on *a priori* or axiomatic truths from
which the rest of mathematics is then deduced as a set of theorems – he maintains that observation is the basis for our acceptance of truths like $2 + 2 = 4$ and ordinary geometrical truths
(however *psychologically certain* we may become of their
truth once we have empirically recognised them), and that

mathematical propositions, like other scientific propositions, are confirmed or falsified by observation of facts.

In the case of geometry, he wrote[2] in defence of his view that considerations of 'pure' or 'rational' geometry in fact depend on 'observations of actuality', and criticised the standard doctrine that, depending on whether we accept or vary Euclid's 'axiom of parallels', we arrive at three different geometries each of which is a 'logically consistent' example of use of 'hypothetico-deductive' method. Now Anderson was loath to make any concessions to the hypothetico-deductive approach and its loose sense of 'consistency', because he regarded it as having no place in formal logic. But suppose we do accept it (as, as mentioned earlier, an extension of his logic of hypotheticals) then we can agree: (1) that if it is just a matter of logical manipulations we can have three sets of 'uninterpreted' propositional forms, and (2) that when these forms are given a geometrical 'interpretation' then, because of the different assumptions made about parallels, we can systematically deduce the theorems of the three 'geometries'. Even so from an Andersonian point of view such a mathematico-logical exercise is parasitic upon our prior recognition of certain basic *empirical* terms and propositions, and so far as the *truth* of the three different systems is concerned, that question is the empirical one of *which* of the varying (that is, *inconsistent*) 'axioms' is in fact true, and consequently of *which one* of the sets of 'theorems' is true. The crucial fact in favour of this empiricist view, Anderson points out, is that geometry is not cut off from, but is obviously connected with physical phenomena; and if, for example, it is possible to *apply* geometrical propositions to physical facts it is also possible to refute them by reference to physical facts. As he sums it up (in a passage that also bears on arithmetic),

It is a condition of our getting to know mathematical truths, and of their having any relation to, any continuity with, other truths – a condition,

---

[2] *Studies*, pp. 6–11. He did not develop his views on arithmetic in print, but for an interesting defence of the view that interpreted arithmetical propositions are empirical see J. L. Mackie, 'Proof', *Proceedings of the Aristotelian Society*, Supplementary Vol. 40, 1966, pp. 23–38.

for example ... of the mathematical having any 'application' to the physical – that they should be discovered in the same situations and by the same experiences as those other truths; and, if this were never so, mathematical truths would have to belong to a different realm of reality from physical truths, and presumably from what is true of ourselves, so that they could never be learned.[3]

Group three:

The category of quantity has both a mathematical and a physical aspect, as it is concerned on the one hand with number, and on the other hand with the solidity and physical continuity of things. So, considering quantity in this latter way, we can establish it as the first category of the third group, and move from it to the category of intensity or degree (as illustrated by the brightness, hardness, etc. of things). Anderson regards this category as involving both qualities and relations, though he denies that qualities proper themselves have degrees and maintains that where certain qualities, such as colour qualities, are confusedly said to involve degrees, what we have in fact are a set of qualities (for example, a set of yellows) that exist in a *range*. In contrast, there are various qualities that do not, in any clear sense, exist in a range – a given man or tree, for instance, is not literally more human or more a tree than any other man or tree. More particularly, examples of this kind differ from qualities like yellow in a further way which involves the interrelation of their parts in a whole. Thus, if something is, say, a human body or is wood it is normally bodily or wooden through and through, and likewise with something that is yellow (at least in respect of its surface). But there are qualities which, while they belong to wholes, are not qualities of the *parts* of those wholes – for example the parts of a human being are not human beings, the parts of a wooden table are not tables, the parts of a yellow rose are not separate roses. Cases of these types thus take us beyond 'through and through' qualities (yellow, etc.) – which provide an empirical equivalent of traditional accounts of *attribute* – and bring us to the category of substance or structure which involves the composition and interrelationships of things. This category, which

---

[3] *Studies*, pp. 171–2.

Anderson likens to the harmony or balance of tensions of which
Heraclitus wrote, embraces both qualities and relations, including Anderson's relations in an extended sense, that is, ones
which involve, as well as strict or spatio-temporal relations, certain specific qualities.

The next category, causality, is similarly a relation in an extended sense in that it involves, along with spatial and temporal
relations, changes in the *qualities* of things. Causality follows
substance as a category because the consideration of a thing's
structure of qualities, parts and phases naturally leads on to the
question of *action* or *influence* on and by the thing. In the case of
causality Anderson, as we saw earlier, agrees with Hume's criticism of the rationalist conception of causal 'powers' but, as
against Hume, he holds that causal situations are whole,
particular–general situations that are open, in single instances,
to observation (and mis-observation). He also connects causality with the Heraclitean theory of exchanges according to which
there is no absolute contrast between change and persistence,
but persistence is a special case of change. That is to say, in some
cases we get a balance of changes in such a way that, although
something *is* being constantly subjected to change, it is not
undergoing any special or notable alteration, and is said to be
the *same*, or a *persisting*, thing or substance. Some other features of Anderson's view of causality, including his conception
of the causal *field* as that which persists while a change occurs,
will be dealt with separately in the next chapter.

Finally, to complete the sequence of third group categories,
we pass from causality to the category of individuality or thing-
hood which concerns the activity or force possessed by everything that exists. For, as part of Anderson's standard criticisms
of the conception of what is a mere resultant or purely passive or
epi-phenomenal he insists that anything that can be produced is
itself capable of producing or acting. This is what is partly conveyed by traditional accounts of substance so that 'substance' in
this (rather special) sense has to be distinguished from the
account given above of the category of substance in the sense of
structure. (This distinction is also relevant to a distinction be-

tween ethics and aesthetics because, as we will see later, in Anderson's view aesthetics is concerned with the structure of works of art whereas ethics is concerned with goods as social forces or activities that interact with other social forces or activities.) At the same time, the category of individuality brings us back to the initial category of identity in that individuality can be said to be a concrete or practical form of identity: it concerns a thing's (or subject's) activity or capacity of affecting other things.

So, summed up, the three groups of categories are:

Group one	Group two	Group three
identity	universality	quantity
difference	particularity	intensity
existence	number	substance
relation	order	causality
universality	quantity	individuality

Anderson's account of Space-Time and its categories is wider-ranging and as such more speculative than other core parts of his philosophy. His deduction and ordering of the categories depends on his equating spatio-temporality, not only with situationality, but with propositionality; that is, with the propositional forms of his logic and then deriving the categories simply from those forms. As such his argument is, as Armstrong puts it, 'one of great philosophical imagination and daring'.[4] It does hold, in broad outline, given our acceptance of his formal logic including its account of the complexity of propositions and of their ingredient terms, as it is by reference to this complexity that, having deduced the first set of categories from the form of the proposition, he can then go on to do so again in the case of the further categories of the second and third groups. However, even if his actual deductions and orderings are regarded as speculative or are treated with caution, it seems to me, at least from a realist, objective point of view, that the categories he cites are, fairly obviously, the categorial factors or features of all situations.

[4] 'John Anderson: On Metaphysics', *Quadrant*, July 1977, p. 68.

A PROBLEM

If we do accept Anderson's precise formal logic there is little to
cavil at in his deductions except perhaps in some of the ordering
details, but there is one issue – about which Anderson himself
worried – that does present a basic problem for his logic and his
overall position. This concerns how, given that position, we can
speak informatively about Space, Time and the individual categories when they are supposed to embrace all things or situations whatever. In Anderson's formal logic and in his account
of significant or informative discourse he holds that propositions
must concern real issues and a condition for this is that the terms
employed must be real and have real *opposites*. But according to
Anderson's theory, whatever is is spatial and temporal, exists, is
caused, etc., yet there is nothing which is non(spatio-temporal),
non-existent, non-caused, etc. How, then, can the terms in
question occur in informative discourse? Now Anderson can,
and does, argue cogently that Space, Time, existence, etc., concerning as they do the conditions of existence and categorial factors found in all situations are not *terms* of his logic – they are not
propositional subjects or predicates – but we can still speak
informatively about them because there are certain genuine contrasts involved. Thus, in the case of Space and Time he argues
that we can speak informatively about them because, as Space is
in Time and Time is in Space, we can specify Space by reference
to Time and Time by reference to Space. Again, in the case of
causality it is because there can be a real issue about whether
something X is not caused by Y that we can, by extension, attach
meaning to the (false) view that X is not caused at all. Similarly,
apparent issues about non-existence have their basis in the fact
that we can wrongly suppose that some *A* are *B* (some mountains are golden, some minds are all-wise, and the like) and so go
on to ask whether non-existent *AB*'s are such and such.

But while we may thus explain, given situational realism, how
conceptions contrary to truths about the categories come to be
constructed, a problem does remain for Anderson. This is that

even though Space, Time and the categories are not in fact propositional terms, nevertheless, in the philosophical statements we
make about them we have to treat them as if they were terms
(existence, for instance, is not a predicate but we have to treat it
as if it were a term when we say 'Existence is a category', and so
on), and if we could not do this we could not expound a theory of
Space, Time and the categories. Similarly, according to Anderson's logic and ontology everything is propositional or situational, but he still has to speak about *propositions* and *situations* in
order to present his own theory.

The issue has affinities with that raised by a principle often
referred to as that of 'polar opposites' or 'excluded opposites'
that has been invoked by some 'linguistic' philosophers. This
principle has sometimes been used in a loose and nebulous way
to lump together quite disparate types of case,[5] but the principle
can be construed in a clearcut, consistent way, namely, as maintaining that universal terms (ones that apply to everything) are
to be rejected as meaningless or at least uninformative.
Expressed formally this amounts, curiously enough, to the position of classical logic according to which for a term-expression
to indicate a genuine term it must have a reference that is both
non-empty and non-universal. So a firm endorsement of the
principle would rule out claims by philosophers to the effect that
everything is 'spiritual', 'divine', 'material', 'caused', and so on,
and ensuing uses of these expressions. In other words, it would
put out of court a great deal of metaphysics and counter-
metaphysics, and solve Anderson's problem about the categories in a decisive way – it would make any theory about them
impossible. However, we can rightly complain that this is an
unsound, not to say cavalier, way in which to look at philosophical problems and arguments. Contrary to it, when in Anderson's
case he maintains (as against the rationalism, idealism, etc., of
other philosophers) that everything is, as a matter of fact,
spatio-temporal, material, complex, knowable, caused, and so

[5] Compare, for example, criticism by John Passmore, *Philosophical Reasoning*,
Chapter Six, and A. J. Baker, 'Universal and Exclusive Terms', *Dialogue–
Canadian Philosophical Review*, Vol. 8, 1969, pp. 84–101.

on, he is adopting a position that is not only meaningful and informative but is one that he backs up with solid and persuasive arguments.

But for Anderson there is still the problem that his formal logic is at odds with his ontology in that the former precludes the kinds of statements he necessarily makes about the spatio-temporal, categorial, and formal features of all situations. The solution of the problem, it seems to me, is to modify his logic by admitting and formalising the fact that there is a logical distinction between ordinary terms and ontological universal terms. This modification is not an extension of formal logic in the wide sense mentioned at the end of chapter six where, by extending the role false propositions have in logic we can admit hypotheticals, unreal terms, etc. The present modification is still realistic and 'Andersonian' in spirit in that it introduces two branches of situational formal logic, realistic and categorial logic, as follows. (1) Ordinary terms are *sorts of things* as Anderson says, and satisfy the ordinary rules of his logic in being real and possessing opposites and having applicable to them the logic of obversion and related implications. This realistic logic rejects ordinary apparent terms like *non-centaur*, and also categorial etc. terms because these are not sorts of things. But (2) we accept it that Space, Time and the categories and the other universal 'terms' employed in statements that deal with the form of the proposition, while they are *not* realistic terms = sorts of things, are nevertheless propositional or speakable. To avoid the ambiguity now attaching to 'term', let us use 'categorial factor' to refer to the new terms and 'categorial proposition' to refer to the propositions in which they occur. Such propositions will have either two or one categorial factors as they will concern either the connections between categorial factors, or the connections between categorial factors and ordinary terms. These propositions have as their formal logic (they are speakable to the extent that there applies to them) the restricted set of implications and logical relationships that correspond to the rules, in ordinary logic, that deal with positive terms but not with logical opposites. This widening of the scope of formal logic, since it involves a formal distinction between the logic of ordinary propositions and that of categorial propositions, does not have the straightforward simplicity of Anderson's earlier system, but it does enable us to find a place in his formal logic of situations for propositions concerning Space, Time, the categories and the formal features of situations.

8

Causality; religion; positivism and linguistic philosophy

> There is no unilinear form of development but interaction at all points.
>
> There is no need to make a special study of Thomism in order to see the unsoundness of a rationalist position which distinguishes 'necessary' from 'contingent' beings instead of recognizing that *anything* is 'necessary for' something and 'contingent on' something.
>
> Linguistic is a substitute at once for philosophy and for a real theory of language.

Several important segments of Anderson's philosophy remain to be discussed. Of these, his social, ethical and aesthetic views will be outlined in the next chapter, while in the present chapter I will elaborate his account of causality and sum up his criticisms of religious doctrines and his view of two influential philosophical movements contemporary with his own.

DETERMINISM

Anderson is a determinist, though a pluralist determinist, for he rejects the monistic conception of causal *chains* and draws attention to the need to make a complex analysis of causal sequences, including making use of the conception of a causal *field*.

The general principle of causality – that every event or situation has a cause – is something, it will be evident, that is entailed by Anderson's theory of Space, Time and the categories. The principle, that is, he takes to be recognised by us as part of our general recognition that situations, as spatio-temporal, have certain regular *ways of working* or *both determine and are determined by* other situations. His argument for determinism, in the first place, is thus that it is something the truth of which we directly observe in our observations of the nature of situations. But in addition, he points out, we may argue indirectly in favour of this observed principle of causality by showing the illogicality of opposed views, including notably the indeterminist view.

Against that view, Anderson points out that indeterminists are unwilling to try to maintain complete indeterminism, that is, the position that nothing at all is caused, and instead hold that things are caused in some ways and uncaused in other ways, that is, that there are two realms, one of determination and one of freedom or indetermination. But this division of reality is open to objections similar to those that confront other dualist positions. First, if the undetermined realm has no influence on the determined realm (if 'free will' has no effect on 'nature') then it becomes a mere nonentity, and, of course, most indeterminists are anxious to maintain that there is an interaction between the two sides of the dualism and that, in particular, the free or undetermined factor can intervene in other areas. But that view is falsified by 'the impossibility of combining the free and the determined in any situation';[1] for if we have an ordinary physical uniformity, A always gives rise to B, say, we have to suppose the existence of a non-uniform factor such that A will give rise to B *unless* free factor F intervenes. But we can have no knowledge whatever of the conditions under which F *will* intervene (for that would be to treat it as, after all, subject to conditions); consequently, F remains a factor that may intervene arbitrarily or miraculously at any time, so that the uniformity is completely nullified – which reduces us to the position of complete indeterminism. The conclusion to be drawn is thus that the existence of uniformities entails that there are *no* non-uniform factors of the kind supposed by the indeterminist.

CAUSAL FIELDS

Anderson's view of the pluralist character of causality is illuminated by another of his original conceptions – that of the causal *field*. This conception, which we have already encountered in

[1] *Studies*, p. 124.

connection with his treatment of hypotheticals, when it is
applied to concrete examples of causal sequences 'enables us',
as he says, 'to make the theory of causality precise and to clear
up the difficulties in which Mill and others are involved'.[2]

Thus, ordinary accounts of causes and effects or of conditions
necessary and sufficient for the occurrence of certain phenomena usually ignore and fail to specify what it is that is subjected
to causal influence and comes to undergo change. It is not just a
matter of a cause C giving rise to an effect E but also of the presence of a field F, which to begin with is not E but as a result of
the operation or introduction of C comes to have the character
E; as happens, to pick obvious examples, when heating makes
cold *water* warm, a stone hits a *windscreen* and breaks it, a cold
virus makes a previously well *man* ill. In everyday cases there is
often a looseness or flexibility in our understanding of what is
the field vis-à-vis the cause and a consequent possibility of confusion, but that can be avoided if we take care to specify just
what the field is. For instance, when we say as we normally do
that a person's operating a light switch causes a light-bulb to go
on, that is correct if we take the field (1) to be the whole electri-
cal situation: the unlit bulb, all the wiring, the source of power
from the main, etc. However, if we treat the power coming from
the mains as also part of the cause, we are then restricting the
field (2) to the unlit bulb and the conduit leading to it from the
switch.

Now the notion of the field can be helpfully enlisted to deal
with such standard problems as whether it is correct to say that
the *one* cause has the *one* effect, or that a set of conditions is
necessary *and* sufficient for a certain effect, or whether, in contrast, Mill is correct when he speaks about the *plurality of
causes*, that is, of a number of precedent conditions *each* of
which is sufficient for a given effect. As Anderson points out
there are a number of weaknesses in Mill's account of causation
and in his methods, including his rationalistic assumption that
situations can be analysed into a number of simple factors, or
that there may be only *one* feature common to compared situ-

[2] *Studies*, p. 130.

ations; but, in particular, Mill's account suffers from its neglect of the field. Thus, when we speak, as Mill does, about there being various causes of death it is unclear what we are talking about until we specify the *field* and also what *exact effect* is in question. For example, what is necessary and sufficient for the death of a human being differs from what is necessary and sufficient for the death of an elephant or of a mouse, and what is necessary and sufficient for the death of human beings of different kinds (young, old, already sick people, etc.) may well be different. That is, there are different issues raised depending on exactly what the field is. Similarly, in the case of effects, differences may be glossed over when we speak loosely about the plurality of causes. Thus a man may die of coronary occlusion, liver failure, or drowning, but these involve different *special* effects, and such special effects (which have different special causes) are different from what is common to them all (men's dying), and the cause of this is customarily regarded by medical scientists as involving heart or brain failure, that is, something common to the various special types of causes of special types of death.

Armed with this approach to the problem, we can uphold the principle that the same sort of cause always gives rise to the same sort of effect; that is, that it is always a matter of necessary *and* sufficient conditions as against the view that there is a plurality of causes in the sense of various conditions each of which is *sufficient on its own* for the effect. The same sort of cause, acting on the same sort of field, is necessary and sufficient for the field's having the same sort of effect.[3] But there is another 'plurality' in respect of causes, fields and effects that may arise. Thus, (1) the same sort of cause acting on fields of different sorts produces effects of different sorts (as when the gin, with which W. C. Fields laced the baby's bottle, affected Fields and the baby differently), (2) different sorts of causes acting on fields of the

---

[3] There is a certain plurality here because, as Anderson says, 'on the theory of the infinite complexity of things, there will be various *necessary and sufficient* conditions of anything', *Studies*, p. 128. However, this does not affect the general principle in question as the various such conditions will all be necessary and sufficient for *one another*.

same sort produce effects of different sorts (as when my consuming a quart of Parker Rough Red and a quart of milk have different effects on me), and of course (3) causes of different sorts acting on fields of different sorts produce effects of different sorts. The notion that effects of the same sort can be produced by causes of *different sorts* – that is, acting on fields of the same sort – is made plausible by a confusion about which effects are in question, but can be removed by specifying which causes, fields and effects are being referred to.

A similar specification enables us to deal with cases of phases or successions, such as the 'ages of man', or the alternation of day and night, where, although causality is involved, we do not say the earlier occurrence is the cause of the later one. To say, for example, that night is the cause of day is equivalent to saying that a region's not being illuminated by the sun is the cause of its being illuminated, when, of course, as Anderson points out,

Taking 'regions of the earth's surface' as the field, we find that the acquisition of the illuminated character (and similarly of the unilluminated character) is the rotation of the earth in relation to the sun's rays; or, if we include the rotation in the specification of the field, we have simply the sun's rays as the cause.[4]

The field also has a significant part to play in Anderson's account of the verification of the truth of propositions including scientific hypotheses. In his general view there is a logical affinity between proof, explanation, prediction and verification. If two true propositions p and q imply a third, r, we have a proof that r is true; they also explain r; and if we have the information in advance that p and q are both true we can correctly predict r. In the case of verification (in the sense of confirmation), given similarly that p and q imply r and the information that q and r are true, then these verify p (and likewise given p and r these verify q); but here the position is that no amount of verification provides us with *proof*. In other words, the obtaining of verifications, no matter how numerous, is quite *compatible* with obtaining falsifications. But what science and common sense

---

[4] *Studies*, p. 134.

find to be useful cases of verification are cases where there are numerous verifications and a complete absence of falsification. Now, in seeking verifications we pay attention to *negative* instances as well as positive ones and it is in this connection that the field is important. If, say, we have the proposition *All men suffering from malaria are men infected by the Anopheles mosquito*, we can verify it by finding positive instances of men suffering from the disease who have been infected by the mosquito, and also by finding negative instances where both factors are absent. But the latter type of case has two forms corresponding to the distinction, in Anderson's formal logic, between the ordinary contrapositive and the virtual contrapositive of a complex *A* proposition. Of these, reference to the contrapositive gives us an immense range of negative instances. Thus, the proposition in the example is equivalent to its contrapositive *All non-(men infected by the Anopheles mosquito) are non-(men suffering from malaria)*, and this is verified each time we find something (a table or a chair, for instance) that is neither a man infected by the mosquito nor a man suffering from malaria. Consequently, in testing hypotheses about causes and effects or about co-existing properties, we find it more helpful to confine ourselves to negative instances in a *field*, – in the example by finding verifications of the proposition's virtual contrapositive *All men non-(infected by the Anopheles mosquito) are men non-(suffering from malaria)* – that is, where we are concerned with the field *men*.

It will be evident that monistic conceptions of causality, including appeals to causal *chains* and related accounts of prede-termination etc., cannot be sustained given Anderson's theory of causal complexity and interaction – which, he notes, 'may as fitly be called "classical" as any theory of single-track develop-ment.'[5] Thus, contrary to the view that there is a single, transi-tive chain of causes, A causes B, B causes C etc., reference to the field discloses that there is complexity and the possibility at every step of contingent and unforeseen developments as distinct from 'pre-ordained' ones. A does not simply cause B, B

[5] *A.J.P.P.*, Vol. 15, 1937, p. 80.

simply cause C, and so on; what we have is (1) A causes X to become B, (2) B causes Y to become C, and so on, and whether or not we say, for example, that A causes C is not inferable from (1) and (2) but depends on what exactly the field that becomes C is. As an illustration consider the case of the familiar nursery rhyme, 'For want of a nail the shoe was lost, for want of a shoe the rider was lost, for want of a rider the battle was lost, for want of a battle the kingdom was lost, all for the want of a horse-shoe nail.' Here the loss of a nail may be said to cause the *horse's hoof* to lose its horse-shoe, the loss of the horse-shoe makes *the armed rider* ineffective in battle, and so on – that is, in each case a different field is involved. Consequently, when it is concluded that the battle (and so, given a further field, the kingdom) is lost because of the loss of a single horseman, that is not entailed by the preceding causes on their own but depends on a further field being, as a matter of fact, present, namely, that *the two armies are evenly balanced down to the last armed rider.*

RELIGION'S ETHIC

Anderson is critical of religion on both ethical and logical grounds. In accord with his positive theory of ethics (which will be described in the next chapter) he regards Christianity, in particular, as essentially servile and philanthropic in its outlook and preoccupations – he here agrees with Nietzsche – and so as quite opposed to what is intrinsically *good*. As he puts it in one formulation:

In my own view, the Christian ethic, as an ethic of renunciation and consolation, as holding out to the lowly on earth the expectation of 'elevation' in some unearthly sense, stands low in the scale of moralities; and I should argue that the Christian emphasis on the individual and his salvation is inimical to a sound view on social affairs, to an understanding of the achievements of the human mind in science and art, which are essentially co-operative.[6]

A further feature of this ethic of servility, he argues, is the

---

[6] 'Religion in Education', in *Religion in Education*, published by the New Education Fellowship (N.S.W.), July 1943, p. 30.

credulous attitude towards inquiry it encourages, as is shown by the kind of bad philosophy – notably subjectivism and reliance on the argument from authority – which Christians draw on in an effort to provide 'evidence' for supposed religious truths. A notorious illustration is the habit university religious societies have of placing emphasis on the activity of *testifying* instead of on making an objective study of religious beliefs. Connected with this is the prevalence of popular 'modernistic' arguments about 'religious experience' which – it is not difficult for Anderson to argue – have the same illogicality as other rationalistic arguments based on supposed indubitable 'experience'; for the Christian, when pressed into making definite, informative statements, has to *characterise* his experience in a specific way, he has to maintain at the least that he is having an experience of X, and in that case he is asserting something empirical and open to possible question, even when he is saying something untoward and mundane, let alone when he is claiming that he is experiencing, for example, 'Jesus Christ'.

Anderson's objection to the credulity promoted by religion is at the heart of his criticism of religious education – which, when he voiced it in an address in 1943, led to a celebrated public controversy. His view of education, in the schools and at the university level, is that it is essentially concerned with inquiry and critical thinking.[7] It follows that religion, in its dogmatism and setting limits to inquiry (setting up that which must not be criticised and the like) is flatly opposed to education. As a result, he took the view that if religion as such is to be taught at all in the schools, it should be taught in a critical and 'controversial' way, that is, by giving an account of opposed religious and atheist views and arguments. But he was more in favour of the pro-

---

[7] It may be noted, however, that he did not believe it is as easy to become a critical thinker as some educationalists (especially nowadays) assume. Compare his comment: 'The hackneyed phrase "thinking for oneself" obscures . . . the field, and the tradition within the field, to which the student must be introduced, and within which doctrines must be set before him in great detail before there would be any question of his "thinking for himself", of his rising above a journalistic level to that of the recognition of types of problems and of solutions', 'Religion and the University', *The Australian Highway*, 1961, p. 50.

cedure of treating religious writings as a part of *literary* studies; though in that case the religious literature studied should include the Greek legends, 'which', he writes, 'have always seemed to me much more interesting than the Christian stories – perhaps because they are connected with the life of a highly cultured people.'[8]

It should be added, however, that in Anderson's view religious education is not as much an enemy of genuine education as is the whole trend (evident in his time and more pronounced today) towards *utilitarian* policies in education. Moreover, on the question of the general social role of religion, while that role is mainly one of fostering illusions, nevertheless in his view religious institutions do have some value in helping to maintain a pluralistic society: as independent institutions they can help to keep up resistance to the ever increasing encroachments of the 'servile State' (as is illustrated by the Polish church at the present time).

ATHEISM

Anderson's view of the *doctrines* of religion is brought out in his trenchant criticism of its traditional theistic assumptions and arguments. In his view, fashionable newer attempts at religious justifications such as those made by appealing to 'religious experience' or to the special character of 'religious language' – the latter involving an attempt to protect religion by maintaining, illogically, that it can only be criticised *within* its own language – are less worthy of serious philosophical examination. They are, one can insist, examples of attempts to promote religious belief by what amounts to the technique of 'soft sell' in that such approaches inconsistently evade, or try to hide the existence of, the key issues – which are at least explicitly discussed by traditional theologians and metaphysicians – namely, ontological issues about the supposed nature of God or the necessary or supernatural order of being.

Anderson, of course, upholds atheism, though that is a rather narrow and negative way of describing his position given its

[8] 'Religion in Education', p. 31.

sweep in rejecting all rationalist conceptions of essences and on-tological contrasts in favour of the view that whatever exists is a natural occurrence on the same level of existence as anything else that exists. From that position it follows, not merely that the traditional 'proofs' of the existence of God can be criticised, but that the very conception of a God or a supernatural way of being is an illogical conception – God is an ontological 'category mistake' as we may say. Thus, the supposed division between the supernatural and natural orders is subject to all the criticisms of ontological dualism, or else (parallel to the replacement of Cartesian dualism by idealism) this dualism is regarded as being superseded by a monism in which *everything* is claimed to be divine or supernatural – which, as Anderson puts it in terms of the propositional copula, is equivalent to qualifying the copula and maintaining that things go on in a *divine* or *godly* way, when all that this amounts to is that they *occur* so that the reference to the divine is otiose.

The three traditional arguments for the existence of God are the ontological argument, which maintains that the very idea or concept of God entails his existence; the cosmological argu-ment, according to which there must be a necessary being, God, on whom depends the contingent order of being; and the argu-ment from 'signs of design in the universe' to the existence of a divine designer. In line with the criticism mentioned above, Anderson points out that each of these arguments is an *ontologi-cal* argument, in that each of them presupposes a rationalistic contrast between supposed independent and dependent ways of being; while, with regard to the arguments taken separately, he agrees with the classical criticisms made by Kant in the case of the first two arguments and by Hume, and following him Kant, in the case of the third argument.

Anderson's own specific contribution consists in a succinct statement, with some improvements, of Hume's refutation of the argument from design. Only a brief indication will be given here of what Anderson says, which is set out fully and clearly in his powerful article 'Design'.[9]

The argument from the supposed 'marks' of order or design in

[9] *Studies*, pp. 88–100, and *A.J.P.P.*, Vol. 13, 1935, pp. 241–56.

the world to the existence of God as its designer, Anderson
points out, involves starting with empirical observations as
premises and then moving to conclusions which are not
sustained by these premises. Thus, there is an argument from
the existence of human contrivance to that of divine contrivance; but whereas in the case of the former there is a distinction
between what is contrived and what is not contrived, in the case
of the latter it is supposed that *everything* is contrived by God, so
there can be no special marks of design (as is required by the
argument) and the argument merely amounts to a re-assertion
of the cosmological argument claim that everything depends on
God. Again, the knowledge we do have about human contrivance depends on what we happen to know about certain specific
relationships, such as that only human beings produce things of
certain sorts: for example, that all houses are made by men, and
likewise we may know, say, that only birds build nests of certain
sorts. When we do know such relations we can then infer the
human contrivance of some things, the bird contrivance of some
other things, and so on; but we do not have knowledge of corresponding facts in the case of the supposed contriver of all things,
and there is no basis for a corresponding type of inference.
Furthermore, there are the problems (conveniently ignored by
proponents of the argument) that arise with reference to the supposed designer himself; for example, if everything has order or
complexity that has to be explained by the existence of a contriver, then, since the supposed contriver will plainly be a being
with order and complexity it will follow that the contriver himself will have to have a contriver; in other words, even if it were
taken seriously the argument would lead to conclusions unac-
ceptable to the theist.

POSITIVISM

Positivism, as a form of pluralism and naturalism, is one of the
descriptions Anderson is prepared to give of his overall position.

That is to say, he takes it that positive philosophy is concerned, not with *a priori* principles or the application of outside metaphysical standards to things, but with the positive nature of things both in the sense of the objective and (as Comte partly showed) the pluralist nature of things.

However, the once influential modern philosophical movement known as *logical positivism* is one which Anderson regarded as in conflict with genuine positive philosophy. This is because, despite the movement's interest in forcibly rejecting theology and traditional metaphysics and furthering the cause of empirical science, its assumptions and arguments – at least in its earlier flamboyant days – were of a thoroughly rationalistic kind.

Thus the logical positivists' famous search for a *verification principle* to distinguish between 'meaningful' and 'nonsensical' propositions in fact involved a search for rationalist *ultimates* in the sense both of supposing that we can arrive at constituents of facts that are simple or purely particular, and of supposing that the percipient can 'verify' propositions by means of absolutely certain experiences. Compare the tell-tale views of those early logical positivists who suggested that, for instance, both universal propositions and propositions about the past are nonsensical because in neither case can we know them with 'complete certainty' or 'all about' them. Similarly, in Anderson's view, the refutation of traditional metaphysical theses involves their being *argued* against; they cannot really be exorcised by brandishing a supposed verification principle at them. In order to decide, say, whether 'The Absolute is one system and its contents are nothing but sentient experience'[10] expresses a proposition (that is, as distinct from being a pseudo-proposition) we have, in particular, to decide whether *The Absolute* is a genuine term. Just to maintain that there are no propositions that verify the proposition in question is to make the prior assumption that *The Absolute* does not exist – which is mere counter-assertion against the metaphysician. To make good a rejection of his theses about *The*

[10] F. H. Bradley, op. cit. p. 129.

Absolute we have, like Anderson and other critics of idealism, to refute his theses by careful argument.[11]

LINGUISTIC PHILOSOPHY

Logical positivism, in turn, was strongly criticised by later philosophers including the mainly Oxford-based 'linguistic' philosophers, whose members formed a very influential post-war philosophical movement. Anderson, however, was also very critical of views sponsored by this movement, though it must be pointed out that – despite Anderson's strictures – there are in fact some affinities between those views and his own views. Thus, as has been mentioned in earlier chapters, there is the affinity between his realism and the criticisms of sense-data and tacit realism of Austin and others; Anderson and Ryle advanced similar endorsements of Plato's later dialogues; and Strawson's views on classical logic including his view that terms are *presupposed* to exist has some affinities with Anderson's account of formal logic.

Anderson was, however, critical of the *linguistic* approach of Oxford philosophers and suspected that it was their implicit acceptance of a naïve social theory in relation to language that led them, mistakenly, to attempt to solve philosophical problems by *conventionalist* appeals to the use of language. Anderson, that is to say, was not impressed by the technique of settling issues by stating 'we don't say' such and such; for example, with regard to Ryle's characteristic claim that we cannot ask *how long* someone spends knowing something because if he knows it he knows it always, including, for instance, when he is asleep, Anderson's reply is that philosophers must be prepared to *question* usage. Knowing something, he argues, *can* have a definite duration and–while, as a matter of usage, we do not normally register this fact by using the word 'know' – we can do so by using words like 'contemplate' or 'learn'; or by means of longer formulations such as the one Anderson gives, 'We know things while we con-

---

[11] Compare John Passmore's illuminating criticisms, 'Logical Positivism, I, II and III', *A.J.P.P.*, Vols. 21 and 22, 1943 and 1944, *A.J.P.*, Vol. 26, 1948.

tinue to exercise our minds on them, while we continue to grapple with the questions they raise.'[12] And with reference to the use we make of 'know' to refer to what, in a sense, we continue to be aware of when we are asleep, etc., this does indicate certain facts about our ability to retain previously learnt knowledge. But the critical philosopher, Anderson points out, will not be bluffed by the authority of this usage into acceptance, for example, of a passive, storehouse view of knowledge.

Some of these differences are revealed in the criticism Ryle made of Anderson's philosophy,[13] and in the reply Anderson belatedly wrote.[14] Ryle acknowledges Anderson's 'numerous, very cogent, ingenious and original polemical arguments' and that 'Platonic Forms, internal relations and twentieth century sensa, in particular, receive an effective trouncing at his hands', but goes on to criticise him for maintaining such things as the following: his empiricist view that there is no sharp distinction between philosophy and science, that logic and mathematics are empirical sciences, that universal propositions are (Ryle inaccurately writes) 'reports of states of affairs', that ethical goodness must be either a quality or a relation, and that, in general, Anderson's set of categories is so exiguous that there are only *two* of them, quality and relation.[15]

Now Ryle clearly makes some mistakes in his exposition of Anderson and in particular attributes to him belief in 'pure particulars' of the kind assumed in Russell's and Wittgenstein's views about atomic propositions. Apart from that, his criticism consists in the main in re-asserting one side, as against Anderson's other side, in a number of recurrent philosophical disputes. Thus, in the case of logic and mathematics, Ryle is putting forward the standard modern 'empiricist' view that implication and other logical relations and the basic truths of mathematics involve analytic propositions or tautologies that ultimately

---

[12] *Studies*, p. 173n.
[13] 'Logic and Professor Anderson', *A.J.P.*, Vol. 28, 1950, pp. 137–53; reprinted in his *Collected Essays*, Vol. I, pp 236–48.
[14] *Studies*, pp. 171–4 and pp. 179–85.
[15] For this point, compare too Ryle's *Dilemmas*, Cambridge University Press, Cambridge, 1954, p. 10.

depend in some way on language. Whereas Anderson, in accordance with his situational realism, takes the view that implication is recognised in the same way as, and is in a *continuous situation*, with, the propositions it relates, and that if this were not so we could never learn facts about implication; and likewise, with regard to mathematics he argues (as we have seen earlier) that the objects of mathematical study (however abstract they may be) are not cut off from physical facts but have their basis in our observation of those facts.

Again, on the question of whether universal propositions are or are not situations or states of affairs, the principal issue at stake concerns the logical status of singular and universal propositions. Ryle, in accordance with the distinction often made between 'facts' and 'generalisations' or 'data' and 'theories' (or in his own language between 'categorical' or 'episodic' statements and 'inference licences') wants to make an absolute logical contrast between the two types of propositions. But making that contrast, in Anderson's view, depends on having an atomistic conception of 'facts' and of singular propositions, and he takes the view, as we saw in connection with his logic, that singular propositions exhibit generality just as (plural) universal propositions do, and that, when true, both singular and universal propositions are, in Anderson's terminology, 'spatio-temporal situations'.

On the subject of categories, Ryle is mistaken in accusing Anderson of accepting only two categories. As we saw in the previous chapter, Anderson holds that there are numerous categories besides quality and relation, and there is furthermore a vital difference between his view of the categories and Ryle's view. This is that Anderson regards the categories as applying to whatever exists so that *all* the categories are to be found in *any* situation. Ryle, however, (following Aristotle and Russell rather than Kant, Hegel or Alexander) treats categories as *exclusive* types of (linguistic) phenomena. It is this type of approach which leads Anderson to criticise Ryle for what he calls 'the "separatist" or atomistic character of his thinking',[16] in

---

[16] *Studies*, p. 172.

looking for *discontinuities* rather than *common ground* in sub-jects of inquiry. But it can be noted that there are some vari-ations in Ryle's account of categories. Often, because of the use by him (and his followers) of very loose linguistic criteria for what are to count as 'category mistakes', categories multiply endlessly – for instance, even bridge terms ('trump', 'slam', etc.) are said to differ in category, not only from other general types of term, but also from one another. But Ryle at times (in his early and also in his late thought) waives merely conventional or factual distinctions as a source of categories and gives a more stringent account according to which category differences need to be established by careful philosophical argument – for example, 'Time began a million years ago' (unlike, say, the false but harmless statement, 'Test cricket began a million years ago') makes a category mistake because of the demonstrable philo-sophical paradoxes it engenders. This leads to a conception of category errors as being of various general types (but quite limited in generic number), notably ones involving confusions about wholes and parts, processes, universals, abstractions, and relations and qualities; these confusions being typically revealed by infinite regresses, antinomies and other distinctively philo-sophical forms of criticism. And such an approach on Ryle's part, emphasising as it does philosophical argument and the detection of confusions about the categories (in Anderson's sense), it will be seen, is much more consonant with Anderson's way of philosophising.

9
Social theory, ethics and aesthetics

Forms of association are the primary social fact. We should think, then, of social movements not as framed by individuals but as passing through individuals.

The fundamental criticism of the life that is guarded by an extensive system of precautions is that it is a mean and base existence and that it is not of the nature of good activities to be so sheltered.

The realist aesthetician demands that a work of art should have a real theme and that the theme should be properly worked out, that is, in real stages or phases.

SOCIAL THEORY

Anderson's political sympathies went through a number of phases, ranging from sympathy for Communism – under the influence of Sorel's conception of the regenerative, self-help qualities of the working class – in his early days, to vehement opposition to Communist illiberalism in his last years. But what I will outline briefly here is his account (which altered little in the course of his career) of the nature of society, which is a theory of *social pluralism*.[1] Characteristically, Anderson develops his own positive social theory by criticising what he takes to be prevalent false conceptions of society. These, in particular, are the conceptions of social voluntarism, social atomism and solidarism or social monism.

According to the voluntarist conception of society, social conditions are determined and indeed constituted by personal decisions, but, against that, Anderson affirms determinism which, of course, includes social determinism, and insists that such decisions themselves are subject to social and psychological conditions. As he writes,

[1] For a detailed treatment of Anderson's social theory, his ethics, and his political history, see A. J. Baker, *Anderson's Social Philosophy*, Angus and Robertson Publishers, Sydney, 1979.

We do not, in fact, step out of the movement of things, ask 'What am I to do?' and, having obtained an answer, step in again. All our actions, all our questionings and answerings are part of the movement of things.[2]

Social atomism (or social individualism), which is typically advanced in conjunction with social voluntarism, is the view that there really are no social forces except individual persons – or that what pass as other 'social forces' (such as movements and organisations) are social resultants not determinants. But as against that view, that the individual person is the atom or unit of society, Anderson affirms the vital importance of wider social complexes, particularly ways of life, movements and organisations or institutions. Such social complexes or 'forms of social activity' are not framed by individuals but 'pass through' or 'work through' individuals, and it is the study of their inter-relations and changes which forms the true subject of social science.

The remaining view, solidarism, takes society to be a solid or harmonious thing, or a single whole all of whose members have a common set of interests. But, Anderson argues, that view – with which is often associated the illusory conception of a *common good* – neglects the fact of social variety and social con-flict, that is, the fact of social *pluralism*. He allows, of course, that tension and struggle are not the only considerable ingredi-ents of social life. There are many forms of co-operation and social cohesion, but nevertheless, contrary to the solidarist, these are not the dominant social facts as conflict and struggle are permanent important features of society and history. More-over, with reference to the appeals so often made in the public arena to the 'common good' or the 'general interest', in his view their main function is one of socio-ethical obfuscation. Whether they are made by 'reactionaries' or 'radicals' (for attachment to solidarism is spread widely across the political spectrum) they cloak the promotion of some quite special interests at the expense of certain other quite special interests.

In place of these confused approaches to social theory, Ander-

[2] *Studies*, p. 241.

son – under the influence of Marx's historical materialism, but revising that position in a decidedly pluralist way – develops his theory of the variety and interplay of complex, psycho-social forms of social activity which work through individuals. He sees, for example, that such organisations as the State, political parties, trade unions, churches, universities, have characteristic ways of working that capture or control many of the individuals connected with them – as notably happens in the case of the bureaucratic and oligarchic features of such organisations, – though he holds that such organisations also often have other tendencies, other movements or ways of living and thinking working through their individual members, which may be of an enterprising or freedom-loving kind and which struggle against the dominant oligarchic tendencies. In the language used by some philosophers today, Anderson's theory thus rejects 'methodological individualism' and accepts a kind of 'social holism' – though the the latter term is misleading because of its frequent association with *monistic* or *totalistic* conceptions of society such as those of Hegel or Marx. He is better described as a social pluralist or social complexist, as he repudiates the view or implication that society forms some single totality or system or has some 'purpose' or single function, and stresses the role in social affairs of social sub-wholes or complexes in which are found a variety of tendencies, activities or interests, some of which are not only opposed but are simply *irreconcilable*.

This is just a broad outline, a statement of Anderson's view of the social categories, which calls for illustration and discussion in much empirico-historical detail. But without attempting that I will mention a question that does arise about the connection between his social theory and his ontology. Thus, he sometimes proceeds[3] as if his ontological position, that is, his rejection of ontological atomism and monism in favour of pluralism, is *sufficient* for a rejection of social atomism and solidarism and hence for the establishment of the main points in his *social* pluralism. (At one time he even canvassed the view that there is a connec-

---

[3] An example is his revealing apposition, 'Individualism or the postulation of any sort of atomic entity', *A.J.P.*, Vol. 37, 1959, p. 166.

tion between denying levels of existence – 'ontological levelling' so to speak – and social levelling, that is, opposition to social privilege and hierarchies, but he later rightly retracted that view.) Now, given his realist ontology, we can at once rule out social positions that depend on ontological monism such as Hegel's account of the role of The Absolute in history, and we could do the same with any social theory founded on pure atomism. That is, any acceptable realist social theory must be compatible with ontological pluralism. But that would not render it *impossible*, for example, for social atomism or solidarism to be a sound social theory, as human individuals, if they were the units or atoms of society, would not be ontological atoms, and society, if it were a solidarist totality or single system, would not be an ontological one. In other words, if we accept (as I do) Anderson's pluralistic social theory as basically correct, it will be because of criticisms that can be directed specifically against social atomism and solidarism, in the light of social and historical facts.

One other question that needs, for clarification, to be mentioned concerns social policy. Anderson carefully distinguishes between giving an objective account of the character of society and of social change, and advancing programmes to alter society. In accordance with his rejection of solidarism and his emphasis on social complexity he does not equate social determinism with the possibility of large-scale 'intervention' or 'control'. On the contrary, he argues that recognition of social regularities sets important limits to human intervention, and he rejects as illusory the claims made by would-be social engineers (of whatever political complexion) that they have blueprints for an overall 'planned' society. That is, as against Marx and other 'utopians', he argues that owing to the complex and conflicting array and interplay of social forces there are no 'final' or 'totalistic' social and political 'solutions'.

ETHICS

Anderson's ethics is one of the most original and distinctive

parts of his position. Ethics, he argues, has nothing to do with
the questions that have so often been raised by writers and moralists on the subject – questions about Duty or Obligation or
what we ought to do, or other such questions about prescribing
or proscribing, praising or condemning, types of human behaviour. On the contrary, ethics is a descriptive, realistic and scientific subject – he calls it *the science of ethics* – which studies the
nature and operation in mind and society of *good activities*.

A convenient way of outlining this position is to look at the
history of ethical theory from Anderson's point of view.

In his view, while moral philosophy has always been dominated
by normative or prescriptive considerations, some past thinkers,
despite their confusions and their moralism, have recognised to
some extent the existence of an intrinsic quality, goodness.
Thus, notably in Plato's *Euthyphro*, we find Socrates suggesting
a distinction between (1) giving a qualitative account of the
nature of goodness and (2) merely giving a relational account of
it by referring to its being loved, admired by certain people. This
vital distinction was kept alive to some extent in later Christian
thought by an issue about whether, when good is supposed to be
commanded or ordained by God, it is true (1) that God commands it because it *is* intrinsically good, or (2) that it is merely
good because God commands it. In particular, the seventeenth
century English Christian, R. Cudworth, while believing that
good activities were created and willed by God, saw that they
would still have to be good by *nature* and not by *arbitrary* com-
mand of God. However, the standard Christian approach has
been, in Anderson's words, to 'ignore Cudworth's distinction
and *amalgamate* the two notions of "being good" and "being
required of us by God"',[4] while other theorists – including contemporary ones – have set up their own secular amalgamations
of goodness with what they claim is required of, or required to
be commended by, us; and it was only in the case of Moore's
Principia Ethica (1903) that there has been any sort of influential
departure (in part) from the moralistic approach.

[4] 'Religion and the University', *The Australian Highway*, November 1961, p. 53.

That book does contain much material that conflicts with Anderson's views. (Moore argues that good is simple, non-natural, indefinable and known by intuition, whereas Anderson argues that it is complex, natural, definable and known by observation, and furthermore Moore was concerned in the end to endorse a prescriptive ethics.) But Moore's important contention, which Anderson went on to develop in a naturalistic, socio-empirical way, is that past ethics has confused the question of discovering what things are in fact good with the question of exhorting people to be or do good. This confusion Anderson re-describes as an important example of *relativism*. Thus, if we consider everyday things, it is easy to recognise the distinction between, on the one hand, specifying things which are apples, or metals, or have an oblong shape, and studying their intrinsic qualities, and on the other hand *wanting* apples, metals or oblong things and seeking to *bring them about*. These are plainly questions of two different types and to run them together would involve us in the fallacy of relativism. But that is the fallacy which moral theorists regularly commit: they illogically confuse or conflate questions about what things are in fact good and what are their particular characteristics, with relational questions about wanting or promoting goods. Prescriptive ethics, Anderson argues, by proceeding in this way is enabled to gain covert support for its authoritarian claims, because it is made to appear that conceptions like Duty or Moral Sense or Natural Rights have qualitative content – though analysis discloses that such conceptions are really relations masquerading as qualities. So what we have to do is expose relativism in ethics and then, setting aside questions about relations, concentrate on the real subject of ethics: the sorts of thing that are good and their characteristics.

Ethical goods are thus definite, psycho-social forms of activity which, like other spatio-temporal sorts of things, have their own distinctive ways of working and are open to empirical, including historical, investigation. There are noteworthy points of connection here between ethics and social science because, for example, of the way in which the character of social movements

and institutions is affected by the degree to which good activities
are present within them. Indeed, apropos this connection, we
can suggest that Anderson's conception of ethics as itself a
science is too narrow; given his position, positive ethics will have
its own field of study – criticism of past and present moral views,
delineation and analysis of goods – but this ethics, *qua* science,
might be better regarded as a significant *part* of social science.

The chief examples Anderson gives of goods are: intellectual
inquiry, artistic production and appreciation, enterprise or freedom, love and courage. In his account of goods he was also much
influenced by Sorel's views about 'the ethic of the producer' as
displayed, in particular, by the working class (so it seemed to
Sorel early this century) in struggling in an enterprising, self-
reliant and heroic way against the corrupt, servile and self-
seeking morality, that is, 'the ethic of the consumer', that
normally prevails in bourgeois society. In the course of time,
however, Anderson – influenced by the spectacle of the decline
of Soviet Communism into tyranny and of Western Socialism
into welfarism – ceased to share Sorel's optimism about the
enterprising, non-servile qualities of the working class, and
came to believe that most members of that class, like most members of the bourgeoisie, are dominated by 'the ethic of the consumer'. Consequently, he came more and more to regard
goodness as an important but minority force in society, which –
in line with Croce's view that 'history is the story of liberty' – has
to live a precarious existence permanently struggling against
evil.

Anderson did allow a possible realist and objectivist alternative to his own view, namely, that good is not a quality at all but
a *relation*, such as support or advocacy (though in that case, he
agrees, ethics will not be a separate science but a branch of econ-
omics or some other social science). Interestingly enough, this
relational view of ethics has been attractive to a number of
members of Anderson's school who otherwise mainly agreed
with his views, so by way of a concluding comment I will note the
point of view of each side in this dispute.

The issue is primarily one about Anderson's entitlement to

use the word 'good' in the way he does. Those people (like myself) who have adopted the relational view can readily agree that the activities Anderson cites as good activities are indeed *qualities* of certain human activities (and ones of considerable social importance), but will argue that the word 'good', including when used in a moral sense (and not merely in non-moral grading ways – 'good cricketer') is so obviously imbued with relational content (people are so often found supporting, wanting, commending, admiring, and so on, what they regard as good) that it is mistaken – and misleading – of Anderson to seek to appropriate the word 'good' in a qualitative sense. Consequently, so the relational argument will run, while he is quite correct in pointing out the relativism of other moral philosophers, the fact is that after critical scrutiny nothing positive remains of the supposed 'qualitative' good. That conception, although it may initially have more of an air of quality than *duty* or *right*, is just one more case of a relation masquerading as a quality, and when examined a statement of the form 'X is good' can be seen to register the outcome of a process of illusory objectification by means of which, when, say, Social Group A supports or advocates Type of behaviour X, X is made to appear to be something which is universally commendable or deserving of pursuit.

However, Anderson's reply to this is, first, that it is no easy matter to develop coherently such a relational view of good (and for that reason he came in the end virtually to retract the possibility of that view's being an alternative to his own); and, secondly, he goes on to insist that the qualitative conception is itself embedded in traditional ethics. Thus the very plausibility of relativism, he contends, depends in part on a tacit recognition by the moralist of the quality good, so that even Christian writers have some faint recognition of positive psycho-social goods. Furthermore, on the question of how do we learn the meaning of 'good' – which although learnt by observation is not learnt as easily as the meaning of, say, 'tree' or 'red' – he does offer a positive answer. We normally do so, he argues, by connecting goodness with *love* (in a child–parent situation) and having discovered that love is a good we may (though not all people will do so) go on to recognise the other positive goods.

AESTHETICS: ERRORS OF RELATIVISM

If traditional ethics suffers from the fundamental error of relativism, so also, Anderson argues, does traditional aesthetics. In a corresponding way to ethics, the history of aesthetic theory and criticism, including literary theory and criticism, has been bedevilled by a relativist running together of questions about the character of works of art – including their aesthetic worth – with questions about relations between works and their producers and appreciators, and about relations between producers and appreciators. Thus there is, in Anderson's view, a genuine subject of aesthetic science – beauty or the characteristics of beautiful things – but while aestheticians and critics may (like moralists in the case of good) have some sense of objective aesthetic qualities, they very often confuse the study of these qualities with the study of the artist's intentions, or of how he has been 'influenced', or of the opinions of aesthetic 'experts', or of the feelings of pleasure that works of art produce in the people who admire or appreciate them. Consequently, the realist or objectivist student of literature and the arts must spend a good deal of time in the preliminary work of criticising prevailing relativist views so that he can *disentangle* genuine areas of artistic study including that of the positive or qualitative goodness of artistic works.

The conception of the 'pleasing' for example (like that of today's the 'relevant') is a widely ventilated conception; but it is easy to show, Anderson points out, that the aesthetic is *not* the pleasing, for there are variations in what pleases or displeases people, and in any case the conception of the pleasing, including the aesthetically pleasing, is a *relational* conception. Thus, if A is pleased by work X, then even if A happens to be pleased by the aesthetic, we have to ask *what it is in X* that pleases A; the question of A's being pleased is secondary to the true aesthetic question, What are the characteristics of X? Likewise, too, attempts to settle the issues by appealing to 'good judges', or to those with 'aesthetic taste' (as so often happens in writings about literature and the arts) involves an obvious fallacy, the argument from authority. Alleged 'authorities' are frequently in conflict or may all be mistaken, but if what one of them asserts, for example about *Hamlet*, happens to be true, this is not because *he* says so but because he has discovered facts about the characteristics of *Hamlet*; in other words, the primary consideration has to be investigation of the characteristics of works themselves.

Anderson also criticises expressionism, a once fashionable aesthetic analogue of idealist philosophy according to which the artist's mentality or experience is expressed in the work of art and is recaptured by the appreciator when he appreciates the work. But this view, though it seeks to ground aesthetic theory in relational questions about origins and effects, still has to presuppose a primary recognition of *what it is* which the artist creates or which affects admirers or appreciators. That is why, Anderson points out,

The two questions, what happens when a person admires a work of art or regards it as 'good' and what happens when an artist produces a work of art are, however interesting they may be in themselves, quite distinct from the aesthetic question of when a work is 'good' or, more generally, when a thing is beautiful.[5]

On the subject of relations, in Anderson's view – as will be made clearer presently – the quality of aesthetic goodness belongs to those works of art which form a certain kind of coherent or structured whole, and so the study of such wholes will include the study of certain relations: relations between parts, phases, etc., within the works themselves. But what he wants to criticise is the confusion with study of the work itself of outside considerations – the psychology of the artist and its relationship to the work, the effect of the work on its admirers, and the like.

In the case of literary criticism (the same is even more evident with art and music criticism) there is a very frequent failure to discuss clearly the work itself as distinct from mixing that in with

[5] *Some Questions in Aesthetics*, Sydney University Literary Society, November 1932, p. 5.

discussion of the writer or of the effect of the work on the critic. Consider how even informed critics discussing, say, *Paradise Lost*, will refer to the evocation of Satan's pride in the work and mix that in with a discussion of whether Milton himself had to fight hard against pride and so could evoke it well; or of whether, say, Shakespeare, being less prone to pride, could depict it with less intensity. Or, to cite some obvious examples in modern literature, consider how often in the case of such writers as Dickens, Hardy, Kipling, Lawrence and Hemingway, there is in the critical studies an interweaving – as if they were a single topic – of an assessment of their works and an analysis of, or a moral commentary on, their personal characteristics or problems. Of course, 'critics' and their readers are interested in a variety of things and are often more interested in the writers than in their works, but what Anderson is pointing out is that *if* we are concerned with a work and its artistic value – say with Lawrence's *Sons and Lovers* or Hemingway's *The Sun Also Rises* – then the subject of study is the work and *its* characteristics, and not the intentions, neuroses, or whatever, of Lawrence or Hemingway.

Likewise, to mention cases of other sorts, as Anderson argued in connection with Ezra Pound's Italian Fascist sympathies, the quality of a writer's or artist's work is judged by reference to the work and not to his political outlook. Nor is aesthetic goodness tied to any particular kind of motivation: a good writer may be motivated (as perhaps James Joyce was) by a belief in 'Art for Art's sake', but he may write in an effort to resolve his own problems, or merely to make a living. Again, take the controversy which occurred in Australia in 1944 when Max Harris, editor of the Adelaide journal *Meanjin Papers*, was hoaxed when he published the poetry of 'Ern Malley', a fictitious poet whom he believed to be real. Anderson (who, like Harris, took the poetry in question to have merit) argued – correctly from a realist point of view – that whatever were the intentions of the hoaxers, the aesthetic question was concerned simply with the qualities of 'Ern Malley's' poems.

MARXIST AND FREUDIAN 'CRITICISM'

Anderson notes that this kind of appeal to origins or effects as a substitute for study of the real aesthetic issues is also commonly found amongst influential critics outside the conventional stream, namely, Marxist and Freudian writers on literature and the arts. Thus, Communists and other Marxists are well-known for giving a social account of aesthetics, as is shown by their repudiation of 'pure' artistic considerations in the interests of the doctrine that works which deal with the workers, or advance the cause of revolution, are superior to other merely 'bourgeois' works. Now Anderson grants that we can, if we wish, ask which works promote or hinder certain social occurrences and then, in line with our particular allegiances or policies, go on to praise or condemn them. That is, we can take up relational issues in an objective way: Does this novel help or hinder the cause of Communism?, or the cause of religion?, or the cause of radical feminism?, or whatever, but there is nothing aesthetic about such issues. Artistic activity is, of course, a social activity and artistic movements are much affected by social conditions, but Anderson points out it is not the case that the *artistic goodness* of a work of art is assessed by reference to its social character – anymore than, for example, mathematics or chemistry, which also involve social activities and are affected by social conditions, have the truth of their propositions decided by reference to their social origins or effects.

In the case of Freudian writings there has been similarly a pronounced tendency to replace study and evaluation of what is presented in works of art themselves by something else: an account of the psychology – conscious and unconscious – of the artist.

As was mentioned in an earlier chapter, Anderson's overall assessment of Freud's work is that its valuable contributions are marred by a too *monistic* approach, and this weakness is also evident in what Freud and his followers say about art. Thus, Freud's general theory of the artist is that he is a person prone to neurosis and fantasy who only finds a way back from fantasy to 'reality' by creating in his works a substitute gratification of his obstructed wishes. But this theory does not account for the nature of artistic *creation* – the *bad* artist may have a similar psychology – and furthermore the same kind of sweeping principle of explanation is used (at least by Freud's followers) to try and explain too many diverse types of person: the ordinary neurotic, the intellectual inquirer, and the political rebel – as well as the artist! Against this Anderson, in accordance with his social pluralism, maintains that intellectual, political and artistic activities are all separate or independent activities that exist in their own right, even though they may interact with one another or with other phenomena – the artistic, for instance, with economic, political and intellectual phenomena. Moreover, on the specific question of whether the artist is specially subject to fantasies, Anderson denies that he *need* be so subject; maintaining in the case of literature, for example, that there are the two separate cases 'where fantasy (someone having fantasies) is the actual subject-matter of the work, and where fantasy operates as a distorting influence on the work'.[6]

Anderson, however, grants that Freudian theory may illuminate the study of works themselves. For example, the theory of the Oedipus Complex may give us special insights into works like *Hamlet* and *The Brothers Karamazov*, and the conceptions of the super ego, ego and id may be of some use if we are studying Shakespeare's *Henry IV* and *Henry V* (and are also of use in the case of the detective story); while, of course, Freudian theory is very relevant if we *are* studying the psychology of certain writers, such as Dostoevsky, and also in the case of study of the psychology of the reader or appreciator and of why works of certain types are popular (that is, independently of whether they happen to be good works); but it is a mistake to confuse these separate studies with one another.

THE SUBJECT OF AESTHETICS

There are thus, in Anderson's view, a number of possible sub-

---

[6] 'Psycho-Analysis and Romanticism', *A.J.P.P.*, 1936, p. 210.

jects related to the arts that they may be studied in a scientific or objective way: the psychic origin of art, the psychology of artists, the specific intentions of an artist (if they can be ascertained) and the extent to which they are fulfilled in his work, the influence on artists of social conditions, the influence on artists (that is, verified influences as distinct from merely guessed at or accidental associations) of their artistic predecessors, the character of particular artistic movements, the psychological and social effects of works of art, and so on – *and* the nature of works of art themselves. But only the last subject is the subject of aesthetic science.

With reference to works themselves, in Anderson's view none of the arts is representational in its aesthetic character; the goodness or badness of a work does not reside in whether it succeeds or fails to represent something. Neither music, which presents arrangements of sounds, nor the visual arts, which present arrangements of shapes or colours, are as such representational; they do not 'tell a story' or depict feelings (though feelings may be aroused in a *listener* or *viewer*); while in the case of literature it is quite misleading to say that good works 'represent life'. There is representation in some of the arts in a certain sense, namely that in painting a two-dimensional surface is commonly used to depict something with a three-dimensional structure, and literature by means of words presents an account of a set of human actions and feelings.[7] But common to the arts is the presentation in individual works (or at least in good works) of a certain *structure* or the articulation of a certain *theme*. The conception of structure or theme is of central importance for Anderson's aesthetics and that is why, in his theory of the categories, he treats aesthetics as having a special connection with the category of substance or structure. His view is that when a work of art is good it has a definite theme which is worked out in a coherent or structured way. He also relates his view to what Joyce writes in *Portrait of the Artist as a Young Man* about the theory of Aquinas that what is required for a thing's beauty are

[7] That is, literature does so by means of *meaningful* words – the words, as *shapes*, taken artistically, would be examples of (bad) visual art.

'wholeness, harmony and radiance', its being apprehended as '*one* thing, as a *thing*, and as the thing that it is'.[8]

Anderson thus gives a single account of aesthetic goodness; although literature has feelings or emotions as its subject, music has sounds, and visual arts have shapes and colours (he doubts the aesthetic character of 'mixed' forms like ballet and opera), in each case aesthetic worth is concerned with structure, with the arrangement of the parts or phases of the work into a coherent whole.

WHAT ARE GOOD WORKS OF LITERATURE?

So far Anderson's position amounts to a general analysis of what it is to make aesthetic studies. By criticising the relativism of some standard views in the field, he disentangles various psychological, social etc. issues that can be set aside, and distinguishes the theme and structure of works as what aesthetics studies. But having thus cleared the way philosophically for that study, it is a different and further question to find and analyse the specific characteristics of good or beautiful works of art – just as, in the parallel case of ethics, it is a further question to decide what sorts of things are in fact good.

But in the case of aesthetics too, Anderson does have a positive contribution to make. He makes this in his various writings on literature in general and on such writers as Joyce (of whose work he was the first influential champion in Australia), Dostoevsky, Meredith, Melville, Kipling and Shaw. (He did not specifically write about painting or music but it is interesting to note, in view of his emphasis on structure, that Cézanne was a painter and Mozart a composer whose works he especially admired.)

In Anderson's positive view of literature, good works are *classicist*, as distinct from *romanticist*, in their treatment of their material, by which he means us to understand that in dealing with particular entanglements of human feelings such works

---

[8] A study of this Dedalus-Aquinas theory is made by A. D. Hope, 'The Esthetic Theory of James Joyce', *A.J.P.P.*, Vol. 21, 1943, pp. 93–114.

have a definite theme which is developed coherently and realistically. Such a theme, however, is a *specific* theme and is not 'life' in general. Taken even in the widest way, the theme of Homer's *Iliad* is not 'life' but wrath, the theme of *Macbeth* ambition, of *Othello* jealousy, and so on; and the question in each case is how well the theme and its ramifications are dealt with. To be more particular, Joyce's *Ulysses*, for example, in its depiction and juxtaposition especially of Stephen Dedalus and Leopold Bloom, has a well-organised structure built around a definite theme, which is that of *exile* of the self and its search for a way out of exile. As Anderson puts it with reference to Joyce's words 'My hell, and Ireland's, is in this life':

Hell, the self-alienation of the spirit, occurs here and now; it is something that has to be fought through, not something that we can avoid by propitiating human or 'cosmic' powers, not something that we can be protected from. He who remains in the circle of propitiation and protection remains in hell. He alone works through it who rejects the easy ways of escape – nodding at an image, repenting, letting one thing 'stand' for another – the whole system of anti-intellectual pretences. This is the central theme of *Ulysses*, and it is this that the Homeric material (the descent to and return from the shades, contentment with a swinish existence, mock-heroism and so forth) subserves.[9]

On the other hand, in the case of bad works, even if they do have a genuine theme that theme may be set forth in a sentimental, melodramatic, incomplete, or some other artistically deficient way. To use Anderson's words again:

A bad work exhibits heterogeneity or absence of a single theme (as is suggested by Croce) and disconnection. Gaps in the structure have to be bridged over or concealed, and this is frequently done (notably in some of Kipling's stories) by the introduction of the occult or supernatural, in other words, by saying the thing is done, without doing it ... Material is inserted which does not belong to the theme, and instead of having a structure we have a fabrication.[10]

The working out of a real theme, he argues further, involves the *exposure of illusions*. It is a feature of romantic or bad works that they involve the cultivation of illusions, though we have to

---

[9] 'Art and Morality', *A.J.P.P.*, 1941, p. 260.
[10] *Some Questions in Aesthetics*, p. 16.

distinguish that from the depiction of illusions *within works* which, of course, has a definite place in good literature. Since literature deals with human feelings and aspirations, illusions – as exhibited by characters portrayed – constantly provide themes or aspects of themes of literary works; but when we come to estimate whether a work is good or bad the question is whether the illusions are *exposed* in the work. Suppose jealousy is the theme; then if it is properly worked out the illusions associated with it will be revealed for what they are – so that determining the extent to which this is done will be important when we are, say, assessing *Othello*. On this point, in the case of drama Anderson makes a novel contrast between comedy and tragedy in favour of the comic approach. If we take, for instance, Shakespeare's *Hamlet* and his *Twelfth Night*, we find that in the former Hamlet takes his revenge in the end and dies without his own illusions about revenge being fully exposed; whereas with the comedy (although it suffers from not having a single or main theme), the important character Malvolio is shown as forced to see through his pretensions. Thus Anderson's suggestion is that it is with comedy or the comic exposure, rather than with tragedy or the tragic 'resolution' by death, that a full or thorough exposure of illusions is best achieved.

CONCLUSION

In assessing Anderson's general aesthetics, it is not difficult to see the force of his analysis of the different issues confused by relativist approaches, and furthermore the force of his view that when we do examine works of art it is questions about their structure and coherence that are of central importance. But where most dispute will occur is with regard to his claim that questions of aesthetic goodness are concerned *solely* with the characteristics of works themselves. This is because of the profusion of different and competing approaches and principles that are so often regarded as being relevant to 'aesthetic' criticism and evaluation. Even Mackie, in a treatment that owes a good deal to Anderson, comes down on a compromise view according to which *various* aesthetic criteria (success in representation, in expressing intentions, in furthering social aims, etc.) may be employed in evaluating works of art, though he does grant that they are all relational criteria except for the qualitative criterion of 'organic wholeness' which pertains solely to the work itself.[11] But Anderson, an unrepentant realist and objectivist, was not prepared to concede *aesthetic* character to such relational criteria, as in his view the only aesthetic criterion, and the one which is embedded in the classicist tradition and has given continuity to aesthetic theory, is that which looks directly for beauty or artistic goodness in works themselves.

Specific aesthetic theories, in literature or the other arts, are well known for the power they have for provoking disagreements, and Anderson's literary theory is no exception. But that admitted, there is surely much value – at least for those of us who have a realist outlook – in his view that in good literary works we have the articulation of a particular human theme, the coherent development of which includes a realistic exposure of the illusions depicted. That view invites us to look hard at the content and structure of works to find out their exact themes and, in our detailed analyses, to consider carefully – quite likely and rightly with argument for and against – just what it is to convey, with regard to a given theme in a given work, a realistic or non-illusory working out of it. In the special case of Anderson's view on 'the comic', this has encountered the criticism that his approach here is particularly narrow. He put forward that view, of course, in the context of criticising the conventional 'tragic' ending in traditional tragedy, but it is true that he places a good deal of stress on the element of comic revelation and exposure that is found in Joyce's work, and also in the work of other writers such as Meredith. However, in his own literary criticism he is quite prepared to praise such works as Dostoevsky's novels and Melville's *Moby Dick* which are hardly examples of a comic exposure of illusions. But perhaps we can take his observations on novelists like Joyce as hinting at an ex-

---

[11] J. L. Mackie, 'Aesthetic Judgments – A Logical Study', *The Pluralist*, Vol. 2, No 3, June 1969, pp. 3–17.

tended theory of 'comic' excellence according to which the very best works have, and good works which lack it could have profited from having, the element of comic exposure in them.

To end on the subject of the aesthetics is a good way of rounding off this survey of Anderson's general position.

That position emerges as having an overall rigour and systematic consistency that is noteworthy for its lack of strain or forced connections in any of its areas. The realist theory of logic and the proposition is interwoven with the realist theory of the situation and of Space, Time and the categories – supplemented by discussion of the various categories, including universality and particularity, and causality. These theories cohere with, and support and are supported by, the realism (in knowledge), the objectivism, the empiricism and the pluralism. Then, with regard to more special subjects of investigation, Anderson brings out the broad conditions for having a theory of the subject, as of mind, social science, ethics, and aesthetics, and in these cases also presents a positive theory of his own: of mind as feeling, of his social pluralism, of the ethical goods, and of literature.

Returning to the aesthetics, this coheres with the rest of his realism in an obvious way, and has a particular connection with the ethics: because of the sort of objectivism he maintains in both their cases, and because of his view that artistic creation and appreciation are forms of ethical goodness and as such examples of free or spontaneous activities – the kind of activity he indicates in his remark, 'Liberty is the ability to take things artistically, to pursue them for their own sake.'[12] And finally his theory of good literature is closely related to realist philosophy's inquiry into truth. Literature, of course, involves the structured portrayal of individual characters in literary works and so is a mode of presentation quite different from that of objective inquiry and criticism. But good literature, in its realistic concern with the exposure of illusions, has a natural affinity with what Anderson calls the *theme* of philosophy, 'that of objectivism

[12] *Education and Politics*, Angus and Robertson, Sydney, 1931, p. 27.

versus subjectivism, of the issue versus the purpose, of truth versus satisfaction'.[13]

---

[13] *Studies*, p. 137.

Further reading

In addition to *Studies*, there are two more recent collections of Anderson's writings.

(1) *John Anderson, Education and Inquiry*, ed. D. Z. Phillips, Blackwells, Oxford, 1980, which is a collection of Anderson's articles and lecture notes on education. That book also contains essays by Eugene Kamenka, J. L. Mackie and P. H. Partridge.

(2) *John Anderson, Art and Reality*, ed. Janet Anderson, G. Cullum and K. Lycos, Hale and Iremonger, Sydney, 1982, which contains Anderson's writings on aesthetics and literature.

Most of Anderson's articles are listed in *Studies*, pp. 375–8. Some other social and political writings, missing from that list, are mentioned in A. J. Baker, *Anderson's Social Philosophy*, Angus and Robertson Publishers, Sydney, 1979. Early writings by Anderson include sixteen short articles, mainly literary or satirical (mostly written under the name of 'Jude'), in the *Glasgow University Magazine*, 1914–18, of which he was editor in 1917–18.

In addition to the writings by other people already cited in the chapters of this book, writings that deal with or bear on Anderson's work include the following:

Baker, A. J. 'Australian Themes', *Australian Journal of Politics and History*, 1976
    'John Anderson and Freethought', *Australian Quarterly*, 1962
    'Logic and Singular Propositions', *A.J.P.*, 1953
Birchall, B. C., 'John Anderson and The False Proposition', *Dialectic*, Journal of the Newcastle University Philosophy Club (N.S.W.), Vol. 15, 1978
Davie, G. 'John Anderson in Scotland', *Quadrant*, July 1977
Eddy, W. H. C. 'Ethics and Politics', *A.J.P.P.*, 1944
Foulkes, P. 'What Is Deduction?', *International Logic Review*, June 1972
Fowler, F. W. 'Value', *A.J.P.P.*, 1935
Gasking, D. A. T. 'Anderson and the *Tractatus Logico-Philosophicus*', *A.J.P.*, 1949
Gibbons, P. C. 'Heteromerity', *A.J.P.*, 1969

Hope, A. D. 'The Meaning of Good', *A.J.P.P.*, 1943

Kamenka, E. *The Ethical Foundations of Marxism*, Routledge and Kegan Paul, London, 1962

McIntosh, G. F. 'The Category of Causation in Psychology', *A.J.P.P.*, 1935
  'The Relation of Psychology to Philosophy', *A.J.P.P.*, 1935

Mackie, J. L. 'A Refutation of Morals', *A.J.P.P.*, 1946
  'Logic and Professor Anderson', *A.J.P.*, 1951

Olding, A. 'Anderson and Religion', *Philosophical Studies*, 1983
  'Polanyi's Notion of Hierarchy', *Religious Studies*, 1980

Partridge, P. H. 'Contingency', *A.J.P.P.*, 1938
  'Logic and Evolution', *A.J.P.P.*, 1934
  'Modality', *A.J.P.P.*, 1935
  'Progress in Evolution', *A.J.P.P.*, 1935
  'Theory and Practice in the Social Sciences', *A.J.P.P.*, 1945

Passmore, J. A. 'Anderson as a Systematic Philosopher', *Quadrant*, June 1977
  Introduction to Anderson's *Studies in Empirical Philosophy*, Angus and Robertson Ltd, Sydney, 1962.
  'Philosophy and Science', *A.J.P.P.*, 1939
  'Prediction and Scientific Law', *A.J.P.P.*, 1946
  'Reason and Inclination', *A.J.P.P.*, 1937
  'The Making of an Australian Philosopher', *Philosophes Critiques d'Eux-Memes*, Vol. 1, 1975

Prior, A. N. 'The Meaning of Good', *A.J.P.P.*, 1944
  'The Subject of Ethics', *A.J.P.P.*, 1945

Quinton, A. M. 'The Nature of Things', Routledge and Kegan Paul, London, 1973

Reinhardt, L. R. 'Olympian Pessimist', *Quadrant*, April, 1980

Rhees, R. '"Social Engineering"', in his *Without Answers*, Routledge and Kegan Paul, London, 1969

Ritchie, A. M. 'Phantasy and Social Theory', *A.J.P.P.*, 1941

Rose, T. A. 'John Anderson: On Literature', *Quadrant*, July 1977
  'The Nominalist Error', *A.J.P.*, 1949

Rybak, John and Janet, *Map Logic and Other Extensions of Traditional Logic*, published by the authors, Sydney, 1973
  Mechanizing Logic, Sydney, 1983

Stove, D. C. 'John Anderson: The Force of Intellect', *Quadrant*, July 1977

Stuart Watts, G. *The Revolution in Ideas: Philosophy, Religion and some 'Ultimate Questions'*, Hale and Iremonger, Sydney, 1982

Index